For Cheryl, Brooklyn, and Maxwell

The Power of a Promise

Promise

**LIFE LESSONS ENCOUNTERED ON MY
JOURNEY FROM ILLITERACY TO LAWYER**

By Lesra Martin
with Tashon Ziara

iUniverse, Inc.
New York   Bloomington

iUniverse books may be ordered through booksellers or by contacting:

iUniverse
1663 Liberty Drive
Bloomington, IN 47403
www.iuniverse.com
1-800-Authors (1-800-288-4677)

Because of the dynamic nature of the Internet, any Web addresses or links contained in this book may have changed since publication and may no longer be valid. The views expressed in this work are solely those of the author and do not necessarily reflect the views of the publisher, and the publisher hereby disclaims any responsibility for them.

ISBN: 978-1-4401-5908-4 (sc)
ISBN: 978-1-4401-5909-1 (ebook)
ISBN: 978-1-4401-5910-7 (dj)

Library of Congress Control Number: 2009932775

Printed in the United States of America

iUniverse rev. date: 8/28/2009

Contents

Introduction

"Mr. Martin, how did you go from being illiterate at the age of fifteen to becoming a lawyer? How did you go from a Brooklyn ghetto to luxurious hotel suites in Beverly Hills and private plane rides with Denzel Washington? How did you do that?"

Those questions were posed to me not long after I had the incredible opportunity to address the United Nations on the importance of literacy and just as I was leaving a speaking engagement where I had been sharing the story of my own struggle to learn to read and write. They came from an earnest young man who couldn't have been more than twelve or thirteen years old, and they caused me to literally stop in my tracks and reflect on the true underlying source of my success.

- *Where **does** a teenager who has never experienced life outside the ghetto find the wherewithal to become a lawyer?*

- *How in the world could an illiterate fifteen-year-old possibly be ready, willing, and able to attend a university just three years later?*

- *And how does a young person who has grown up surrounded by gangs, violence, and addiction manage to not only make a success of his own life but also inspire others to do the same?*

Many people think our circumstances are the greatest determinant of the life we will have. I disagree. Some people are born with every possible advantage and still live their entire lives without ever recognizing the opportunity that has been given to them. Likewise, others are born into the most difficult of circumstances; yet, because they are able to see the potential that lies within them, they build on what they have to accomplish great things.

The good news for all of us is that circumstances themselves don't predetermine anything. They provide us with nothing more than the motivation to succeed or an excuse for not trying—depending on how we use them. In the end, it is our attitude toward our circumstances that makes all the difference in the world, and thankfully, that is something we alone control. My discovery of this simple but profound truth—and how I was able to use it to change my life—is what *The Power of a Promise* is all about.

Each one of us has the potential for a great life. Each of us has something special to offer the world; we need only to discover what it is. If you take the time to read and apply *The Power of a Promise,* I hope you will discover the life that you were meant to have and the gifts you have to share. As you will notice, the book centers on six important elements that provide focus in my life and guide everything I do. They are hope, heart, human spirit, dreams, determination, and discipline. The significance of each one of these elements is demonstrated in the stories I have included in the corresponding sections of the book, and they are further elaborated on in the twelve promises that conclude each chapter. It is my belief that these elements provide a solid foundation upon which we can all build.

As we embark on this journey together to discover *The Power of a Promise*, I want to thank you for giving me the opportunity to share my story. I wish you much success.

Part 1
Hope, Heart, and Human Spirit

Life presents us with many challenges, testing our strength and inner capacity for growth. While problems and difficulties will no doubt come our way, one thing I have learned for certain from my experiences is this: even in the darkest moments, a glimmer of *hope* always exists, and with our god-given talents, there is no greater force than the power of *heart* and *human spirit* to overcome adversity—if only we choose to use them. Our ability to harness these three elements and put them to work in our life is what will either "make us or break us," as my mother would often tell me.

- *Hope.* Without hope, there would be no achievements in the world, for nothing would ever be attempted. Every endeavor takes its life from a glimmer of hope. Hope enables us to believe that anything is possible. Hope is a state of mind that gives us ability and encourages us to work for something. Find your source of hope and begin the journey to achieve your full potential.

- *Heart.* The heart is a muscle: the more we use it, the stronger it grows. Let your heart be your guide. Although the answers we seek to help us face the challenges and overcome the obstacles we encounter along our journey may not be obvious, the solution is always within. In times of uncertainty and doubt, don't give up on your goal. The heart has reasons that reason cannot comprehend—let your heart be your guide.

- *Human Spirit.* The spirit that resides deep within each one of us is a stranger to both fear and failure. Spirit provides us with the ability to get back up and keep fighting no matter how many times we have been knocked down or counted out. Human spirit knows but one thing—how to try. If you've ever watched a young child attempt to tie a shoelace or zip a coat, you will know this to be true. The human spirit drives us to keep trying, again and again, until we achieve our goal. Thankfully, we don't lose this ability when we grow up. Tap into the power of the spirit within you.

Life is a special gift. We all have a trail to blaze and the ability to achieve great things. As you work to be the best you can be, allow hope to be a beacon of inspiration, particularly when your way becomes clouded by despair or indecision. Let your heart guide you around the obstacles that would trip you up and the detours that would send you down the wrong path. Find strength in the human spirit that lives within to pull you through the difficult moments when hesitation and doubt might trick you into giving up. With hope, heart, and human spirit, we all have the power to realize our dreams.

1
Seize the Power: How One Simple Promise Could Change Your Life

There's an old saying, "You can lead a horse to water, but you can't make him drink." That horse was me. I could see the water. Hell, I wanted it so badly I could smell it and taste it—and God knows I was thirsty. But I was afraid that, if I stepped up and took a little drink, all the good things that had happened in my life recently would suddenly evaporate right before my eyes. Logically, I knew that the opportunity of a lifetime lay within my grasp, so why was I still too paralyzed to make the leap of faith?

I was spinning my wheels, and I didn't know how to stop. Every morning the pattern was just the same. From the moment my brain emerged from a dream state into consciousness, a flood of negative thoughts took over. Even before I put a foot on the floor, I found myself overcome by an overwhelming feeling of exhaustion.

Although some part of me realized that I was the one putting up roadblocks and hurdles—mostly because I felt unworthy and intensely guilty about leaving my family behind in the ghetto while I escaped—I couldn't seem to stop myself. It was as if I were playing a tape of my life on rewind all the time, going over and over all the bad things that had happened back in New York. As a result I was becoming increasingly worn down and tired of the struggle.

3

Finally, after months of struggling, I woke up one morning and decided that I couldn't do this anymore. I was fed up with being tired. I was worn down and exhausted before I even got out of bed. It was time to flip the coin and try something different. I reasoned it this way: if after all this time I couldn't budge or couldn't take advantage of the opportunity, then what did I have to lose by changing my approach? Nothing. I decided right then and there that the next morning I would take a different tack.

"Tomorrow," I promised myself. "When I wake up, instead of allowing all of those negative thoughts to take over, I'm going to replace them with something positive."

Although I was just fifteen years old at the time, I knew instinctively that somehow my salvation lay in my ability to live up to that promise I made to myself in the fall of 1979. As it turned out, I was right.

Just a few months earlier something unexpected had happened in my world—a world that existed primarily within the confines of a three-block section of the New York ghetto neighborhood known as Bedford Stuyvesant or Bed-Stuy as we called it. A group of do-gooders (hippies at that time, but more likely social activists by today's standards) came into my life and literally plucked me out of the ghetto and took me to live in their big fancy house in Toronto, Canada. Their intention was to provide me with an education away from the poverty, violence, and despair that were part of the reality of my everyday life in Bed-Stuy.

I know it might sound more like the storyline from that nineties TV show *The Fresh Prince of Bel-Air*, but that's exactly what happened to me. Despite the fact that it seemed as if all my dreams had been magically answered, I was having trouble dealing with this new reality—which partially explains why I was spinning my wheels. The other half of the equation was that neither I nor my benefactors really understood at the time just how impoverished my education had been to that point and the enormity of the challenge that lay ahead for all of us. Even though I had just completed tenth grade (immensely proud that I ranked third in my class), the cold truth was that I couldn't read or write a single word of standard English—and that takes us back to the story of the promise I made to myself.

Toronto was a different world. The do-gooders who had rescued me lived in a wealthy Toronto neighborhood where the enormous homes that lined the streets were surrounded by wide green lawns and more trees than I had ever seen in my entire life. No smell of urine drying on the fronts of buildings where the winos had relieved themselves. No malnourished kids endlessly throwing balls against the corrugated metal doors that shuttered storefronts. No gang members skulking about looking for someone to prey on.

My life in Toronto was also in stark contrast to the one I had known in New York. In addition to providing me with good nutrition and access to the medical and dental care that had been desperately lacking in Bed-Stuy, my benefactors did all they could to draw me out and introduce me to a larger world. They took time to read books and newspapers out loud. They watched TV news with me and asked my opinion during discussions about their various entrepreneurial ventures. They also took me to libraries, bookstores, art galleries, poetry readings, and other cultural events to spark my interest in learning and provided private tutoring to tackle my illiteracy.

Despite all of the wonderful opportunities that surrounded me, I wasn't responding. Still allowing myself to be tormented by memories and emotions from my past, I continued to give in to the frustration and humiliation I felt at not being able to read and write. That is, until the day I finally decided that I'd had enough and promised myself I would try something different. For the first time on that day, I discovered just how much power I actually had over myself and my life and how the simple act of changing what I focused on could change absolutely everything.

Making a promise to focus on the positive things in my life may have been an easy decision; keeping that promise turned out to be a bigger challenge. That first morning when I woke up after deciding to flip the coin and try something different, I soon discovered that I could only come up with one positive thought (thankfully, it was enough to get me started). I thought about Grandma Costa, an elderly blind lady from Queens who had taken me under her wing a few years earlier and trusted me even though she had absolutely no reason to do so. I thought about how she had believed in me, even when I didn't know enough to believe in myself. So, armed with Grandma Costa's strength, I stepped out of bed ready and willing to meet the challenges that lay before me for the very first time since my arrival in Toronto.

5

The next day wasn't much easier. I dug around in my mind for a new idea and thought about Sam, the bar owner who had brought me into his life in much the same way as Grandma Costa had. Sam had allowed me to work in his bar even though I was a minor.

Thinking about Grandma Costa and Sam, I realized how memories of the many bad things that had happened to me and my family in the ghetto, coupled with a strong dose of survivor's guilt (why did I deserve to get out when my siblings hadn't?) had been conspiring in my mind to keep me paralyzed. The thought that finally got me moving was realizing that one after another good people, including Sam, Grandma Costa, and now these do-gooders from Canada, had offered me a hand up. They all believed in me—and now it was time for me to say, "Okay, let's take the hand and see what we can do."

In those first few weeks of focusing on my promise, I'd like to say it got easier to come up with positive thoughts, but it didn't, so I found myself replaying the few positive images that I had over and over again. Although I was still haunted by some of my most pressing fears, such as worrying if my little brothers would have anything to eat that day, I began to have some faith in myself and focus on the opportunity I had been given to make a better life.

As I made progress, I also began to replace the positive thoughts from the past with situations from my present. It was this growing reservoir of positive experiences that eventually helped me to bridge the gap between my past and present reality. As a result I began to change my perspective and my outlook. I started to recognize positive things around me and to appreciate the miracle that had happened to me. All because of one little promise, suddenly I felt differently, I looked at the world differently, and I began to act differently. This realization literally changed my entire being—and my prospects for the future.

As I was growing up, my mother always said, "You have to dress for the job you want, not the job you have. You have to think for the life you want, not for the life you have."

Making that promise to myself helped me to start to focus on where I wanted to be, on what I wanted to accomplish, and on the life I wanted to build.

> *The Power of a Promise is a powerful thing!*

I had been held back by fear. I had been held back by thinking I would disappoint my benefactors or that I would let down my family because I wasn't there to help them. When I finally gained some perspective on my situation by making a promise to focus on something positive, I started looking at my potential rather than worrying about my problems.

> *The Power of a Promise started me on a path to achieving all of my dreams!*

The moment I opened myself up to my potential, magical, wonderful things started to happen in my life. By making that one little promise to myself, everything started to come alive for me, and my dreams became real.

As a result of my promise, I got an education that was second to none and fulfilled my childhood dream of becoming a lawyer. Rubin "Hurricane" Carter became an important part of my life. He was a boxer in the mid-60s, who was unjustly convicted of murder. He was later released, after serving almost 20 years behind bars. His story was the subject of the Hollywood film *The Hurricane*. Because of the production of that film, I had an opportunity to meet actor Denzel Washington and appear on both *The Oprah Winfrey Show* and on *Larry King Live*. The promise helped me discover my passion for inspiring others with my story. I was invited to speak before the United Nations on the topic of literacy. Imagine me, a kid from the ghetto, standing at the podium addressing leaders from around the world—it sounds like something out of a Hollywood film, but this one's based on a true story, and it all started with my ability to make a promise and run with it.

> *The Power of a Promise is within you!*

I'm convinced that making a promise has the ability to change lives. However, I am not a fan of the tired advice, "I did it, so can you." My message is more than that. There's no magic formula. You've got to rely on your own abilities, tap into your inner strength, and keep going even when it feels as if you want to drop to the ground and give up. It's not magic, but it is magical because you alone have the power to change your life.

Promise to Focus on the Positive

The Power of a Promise is the ability to live in the moment and seize all the opportunities that life puts in your path.

We all have struggles. We all have difficulty staying focused on what is truly important in our lives. What we do during those times of struggle, how we face up to our difficulties, and whether or not we are able to refocus on our priorities is what determines our ultimate success in life. One of the biggest challenges I faced in my own life was illiteracy. Little did I know that, in finding a way to overcome my problem, I would discover a valuable tool I could use to tackle all of the other challenges that would come my way.

Discover the Power of a Promise today!

In response to what was truly one of the most frustrating moments in my life, I made a promise to myself to flip the coin and begin each day by finding at least one positive thought to focus on. I soon discovered that changing the way I started my morning had a powerful effect on my attitude and on how the rest of my day went. I also discovered that by choosing to focus on something positive, I was also choosing not to focus on the negative thoughts that had been filling my head to that point. With a clearer head and a more positive outlook, I began to make progress on my goal of learning to read and write. Suddenly, I was off the bench and in the game. I had discovered the Power of a Promise.

Don't discount the importance of programming!

Isn't it odd how, when faced with a challenge, our human nature tends to kick in, causing us to fall back on our programming— what we've been taught or whatever is most familiar to us. That's why it's critically important to get our programming right to make sure that we default to positive, healthy habits.

It's far more common for us to remember our past failures and the negative things that people have said and done than it is to recall the positive ones. That's why it's important that we make a conscious choice to seek out those positive experiences and make a point to give them more play time in our mind—even if there's only one or two to start with.

To change your life you have to change the messages in you!

The human mind is, no doubt, capable of remarkable things. In large part this is due to the power of imagination and the inability of the subconscious mind to differentiate between what is real and what we have made up. We can use this power to help us or hinder us. We can choose to dwell on the disappointments in our life (replaying them over and over like a never-ending horror movie), or we can make our own "highlight reel" of the positive experiences we've had and make them the main feature in our head.

Changing the messages that play in our head is an important part of changing our focus. Often, we aren't even aware of how negative and limiting those messages are. If you want to go somewhere, tell yourself you belong there. If you want to accomplish something, tell yourself you are capable. If you want to move forward in your life, turn that negative voice into a positive one.

Inspiration is all around!

On the day I prepared to write this promise about the importance of having a positive focus, I walked into my chiropractor's office where I happened to noticed a framed inspirational message. It reminded me of the important point that inspiration is all around us. We only need to open our eyes. To illustrate, I would like to share the message with you:

A Smile
A smile costs nothing but gives much. It enriches those who receive without making poorer those who give. It

takes but a moment, but the memory of it sometimes lasts forever. None is so rich or mighty that he can get along without it, and none is so poor but that he can be made rich by it.

A smile creates happiness in the home, fosters good will in business, and is the countersign of friendship. It brings rest to the weary, cheer to the discouraged, sunshine to the sad and it is nature's best antidote to trouble. Yet it cannot be bought, begged, borrowed or stolen, for it is something that is of no value to anyone until it is given away.

Some people are too tired to give you a smile, give them one of yours, as none needs a smile so much as he who has no more to give away.
Author Unknown

Don't overlook the positive influences in your own life!

Whenever I am speaking to an audience, people ask me how we can change our attitude and where to start. I always advise them to think about the positive people in their own lives—those who have been there for them and tried to direct them down the right path—and imagine what they would say. In searching for answers we often overlook the wisdom of the people who have invested the most in our growth. They are the people who love us unconditionally, the ones who believe that we are all capable of accomplishing our dreams—and they want us to believe it too. They pick us up when we fail and encourage us to try again. They are the ones who have faith in our abilities, take the time to show us the strengths we've overlooked, and give us the courage to overcome our self doubt. When we choose not to use what these wise people in our lives have to offer, not only do we diminish our own potential, we also devalue their contribution and waste a valuable resource.

Begin to make promises to yourself!

When I overcame my problem with reading and writing, all of a sudden I had not only physical freedom, but also intellectual freedom. Today, as a result, I have time to think, time to respond, and time to help others. I learned just how significant making a promise to yourself and sticking to it can be, and that is what I want to share with you.

If you are ready to promise yourself to focus on the positive, let me share with you some promises I make to myself each day to help maintain a positive attitude and outlook.

I promise myself today that I will not be deterred by the challenges and difficulties that lay ahead, that I will stay focused and stay positive.

I promise myself today that if I have faith, if I believe, there is nothing I can't do when I set my mind to it.

I promise myself today that I will take hold of the coincidences and opportunities that life can sometimes present to me. I will be ready.

I promise myself today to:

Watch out for those people who will say, "It can't be done," and then interrupt while I am doing it.

Watch out for the tendency that we all have to resist change.

Watch out for that little voice that says, "I can't do this."

And I promise I will remind myself that I will never know what I am capable of unless I make an attempt.

2

Get Ready to LEARN: Live Every Aspect of Your Life Right Now

One of the most important lessons I've learned in my precious years on this planet is that we can never count on tomorrow because we never know what's coming down the road or when our time may be up. That's why I believe it's critical that we're prepared to **L**ive **E**very **A**spect of life **R**ight **N**ow or *LEARN*, as I have come to term it.

Being ready and able to *LEARN* requires the ability to live in the moment. It also requires an ability to appreciate what we've got and realize that our present circumstances are not always an indication of what our future will hold.

My mother always said, "Tomorrow isn't promised to anybody." The one and only promise that we have a right to when we're born is the promise of potential. It's up to us what we do with that potential. We can use it or we can abuse it, we can build something wonderful with it or we can throw it away. It's all up to us, so no matter how bleak our circumstances appear to be, no matter how difficult the challenges are that we face, we have to approach life with an attitude that says this: I'm going to make the best of my circumstances by *starting where I am, using what I've got,* and *doing what I've got to do.*

That's my approach to life today, and it's one I would recommend to everyone, although I have to admit I learned that lesson the hard way—from my own experience. Like many people, there was a time in my life when I was neither ready nor able to *LEARN*. The following story will help to explain why.

When I was twelve years old, my family moved to the ghetto neighborhood of Bed-Stuy. At that point, my father, previously employed as a foreman in a glass factory (he had also been a back-up singer with the doo-wop group the Del Vikings in his younger days), found himself unable to work as the result of a serious back injury. We could no longer afford our modest house in Queens.

Although we'd had our share of ups and downs, our family had always managed to take care of one another and find a bright spot to focus on. Now, with nowhere else to go, we found ourselves—me, my parents, and five of my seven siblings—living in a cramped, nearly windowless railroad flat in one of Brooklyn's poorest districts where it wasn't uncommon to hear bursts of gunfire. The streets were filled with boarded-up storefronts, mounds of disgusting garbage, forlorn shells of rusting cars, and burned-out tenement buildings. We soon discovered that many of the buildings had been burned by their owners to collect insurance money. These tenements now provided shelter to the scores of prostitutes, drunks, and junkies who populated the streets by day but had nowhere else to go when it was cold and dark.

We were caught in a downward spiral. None of us seemed to know how to make it stop. As both my mother and father turned to alcohol to numb their growing sense of despair, and as my older brother Fru became more and more consumed by a life filled with gangs, violence, and crime, as the second oldest son, I struggled to deal with the harsh new realities that had become a part of my everyday life—and now seemed inescapable.

Despite the fact that living on welfare and food stamps meant we often had no electricity or very little food for a week or longer every month, being cold and hungry weren't the worst of my problems. As the new kid at school, the worst reality of my life in Bed-Stuy was that I had become the target of a couple of bullies, Eric and Julius.

Baby-faced Eric was a nasty little fellow with a foul mouth who strutted around school wearing the best clothes, the latest sneakers (most likely stolen), and no one dared to touch him, which told me that he must be paying his way to stay in one of the local gangs.

Scowling, swaggering, he'd pull himself up to look taller whenever he saw me.

"Punk," he'd sneer whenever he passed me.

Although I knew I could probably take Eric in a fair fight, there was nothing fair about Eric's fights. Once he started one, he'd back away and let his gang members finish the job. Worse, his friend Julius, a hulking, malignant presence, was never more than a few steps behind to take care of any "problems" Eric might encounter.

Although I was generally an easygoing kid more likely to walk away than get into it with anyone—or, upon reflection, perhaps because of it—it didn't take long after my arrival in Bed-Stuy before Julius had his attention laser focused on making my life a living hell.

For my sake and the sake of my younger brother Elston, I tried hard not to let my fear show on the outside. When I couldn't avoid being near either Eric or Julius, I walked by with eyes front and my head held high. The rest of the time, I did my best to stay off their radar screen knowing full well that it was only a matter of time before their gang jumped me in the same way I had seen them take down other kids at school. I let fear take over my life!

If you've never felt it yourself, I can tell you that living with the constant fear of being attacked makes you jumpy. After awhile, the desperation you feel can lead you to do things you wouldn't normally do if you had your wits about you. Things like taking my brother Fru's handgun to school the day after I'd had a run-in with Julius in the classroom where he slapped me hard in the face—and threatened more. With the gun stuck into my belt (I didn't have the clip, but no one else knew that), I spent the day showing it around in hopes that word would spread to the gang members that I was someone they wouldn't want to mess with. That ever-present fear led to an incident shortly after my thirteenth birthday—one that almost ended my life. And the truth is, at the time, I would have welcomed the escape.

It was lunchtime. As I stood on the edge of the concrete schoolyard keeping a watch out for Eric and Julius while contemplating what to do, I caught sight of a group of kids playing tag on the roof of a building across the street. Calculating my odds, I quickly decided that the rooftop had to be safer than the schoolyard, so I dashed across the street.

As I caught my breath in front of what was really only the burned-out shell of a building, second thoughts made me pause, but then I realized that something more than fear was pushing me on. An unspoken emptiness had invaded my life. Anger and the accumulation of too many unanswered questions bubbled just below the surface. I barely recognized my parents anymore. Silent and distracted, my Pop had become a ghost of his former self, drifting along in a haze of alcohol. My mother, too, had changed, and her emotional distance and hard words were driving a cold wedge between us. I had never felt more lost in my life.

Inside the dank, unlit entryway, the overpowering stench of urine stung my nostrils. I held my breath as I stepped carefully through the garbage, rubble, and rat droppings that surrounded me to reach the stairs. Taking a step up, I realized that the stairs had rotted through completely, but somehow I knew that the other kids had made it up the five stories to the roof and so would I. I opened my legs wide and straddled the gaping hole over the staircase, wedging my feet against the edges of each step. I clung to the chunks of the banister that hadn't yet given way and shimmied my way up one flight after another. Finally, I burst out on to the rooftop just as the kids were choosing someone to be "it."

"Yo, yo, yo. Can I play?" I called out.

They whirled around and the kid who was "it" brightened. None of them knew me, but as the newcomer, I was automatically "it."

"No jumping from building to building and watch the weak spots in the roof," someone called out the rules as I began to count and the rest of the kids scattered.

"… 8 … 9 … 10!" I finished and tore after the nearest kid. Intent on catching him, I slid over the tar stains, laughing and excited to be part of the game. For the first time since arriving in Bed-Stuy, I felt free.

Getting caught up in the moment, I pushed myself to run harder with arms outstretched, I lunged at the kid who was right in front of me. And then it suddenly dawned on me what he was doing. The kid stopped to crouch and brace himself before springing into the air and jumping the five-foot gap between the buildings. Pitched forward by my own momentum, I couldn't stop. I flew past the edge of the roof.

Oh, NO! I thought, incredulous that the other kid had jumped. *Oh, God, I hope I make it,* I prayed, cursing at the same time.

The boy I had been chasing landed on the next rooftop with barely a foot to spare. He turned and stood frozen in place as he watched me land behind on the very edge of the rooftop and literally rock back and forth, helplessly flailing my arms. For a split second, I wobbled on the ledge. Then the bricks began to crumble beneath my feet. I slipped down the face of the building. Catching the ledge with my fingers at the last moment, I managed to haul myself back up to chest level. But no sooner had I done that than the bricks I was clinging to disintegrated into chunks as they pulled free.

I don't remember falling to the ground five stories below, but I came to, face down on a pile of bricks. I struggled to push myself up with my arms, but they collapsed beneath me. I opened my mouth to cry out for help, but all that came out was a strange croak. Unbearable white-hot pain shot through every part of my body. The metallic taste of blood mingled with the grit in my mouth. I closed my eyes, not caring if anyone helped me or not. *Why bother?* I thought. I wanted to die. I felt as if my life had already ended months before.

Although I was fading in and out of consciousness after that, one thing I do recall is the voice of one of the ambulance attendants saying, "There's no way this guy is alive. We'd better call the coroner."

The next moment everything turned black as they casually dropped a blanket over my head.

At some point, I must have twitched beneath the blanket because one of the attendants yelled, "Holy Mother of God! He's still alive!" Suddenly they were rushing to get me onto a stretcher and into the ambulance.

I was alive, but I wished I had died.

The story in our family is that my name came from the Bible and is a combination of Lazarus (who rose from the dead and was blessed with the gift of life once again) and Ezra, a famous scribe and priest. My father's gentle southern drawl softened the combined names into Lesra, and it sounded just right.

Some would say fortune smiled down on me that day in Brooklyn. Miraculously, I was still alive. But to me at that time, there was nothing miraculous about it. Anger boiled inside of me. The paramedics and hospital staff had saved my life and treated me

17

kindly. But I hated them for that. They were keeping me alive only to throw me back into the chaos I desperately wanted to escape. Death would have been kinder. I hated myself too for letting the ambulance attendants know I was still alive when I twitched my hand. It would have been better to let them think I was dead, to lie completely still under that blanket, and to let the life drain out of me as I lay on that pile of rubble.

Everyone said I should have died after my body was crushed lifeless in that five-story fall. Yet, like Lazarus, I had been given another chance to live even though I no longer believed the life I saw before me was worth fighting for. My circumstances were governing my attitude. As a result, I had given up on life.

Ironically, it would take another fall many years later for me to realize just how precious the gift of another chance at life really was and to understand the importance of being ready to *Live Every Aspect* of my life *Right Now*.

My second brush with death happened when I was thirty-five. Newly married and in the process of settling down in the friendly community of Kamloops, British Columbia, where I had recently been hired as a Crown Prosecutor (similar to a District Attorney in the U.S.), I was excited about the future. To celebrate my new job and also as an opportunity to get away for a few days and enjoy British Columbia's great outdoors, I planned a weekend camping trip with some old friends.

Arriving at the campsite, we diligently set up our tents and, being responsible campers, also placed candles around all of the tent pegs (just as you are supposed to do). Our work done, we strolled around the camp grounds just as the sun was setting to meet our neighbors, who by this time of the evening were sitting together singing and strumming a guitar. They invited us to join them.

Wanting to grab a bottle of water before sitting down by the campfire, I ran back to our campsite in the growing darkness and guess what happened next? That's right, not more than an hour and a half into my camping trip, and after going to all the trouble to take safety precautions, I stumbled and tripped over a tent peg. WHAM! Down I went, hard, with my head hitting the ground. I was *down* for the count. When I came to, I tried to get up, but I couldn't do anything more than lift my upper body. And then back down I went, hard to the ground and blacked out again.

It may sound strange to you, but even though I'm sure I was unconscious at the time, back in the recesses of my mind, I could hear my own weak, frail voice willing me to move. *Lesra, you've got to get up,* it said. *Lesra, come on, you've got to get up!* As I slowly started to come around, the only thought that kept going through my head was, *Is this it? Is it all over for me?* I was scared, but I knew that if I wanted to survive, I was going to have to fight the urge that was washing over me, the urge to just give in right then and there. *This can't be it,* I told myself. *I still have too much I want to do.* This time was different. I had everything to live for.

I willed myself back into consciousness and staggered up to find my friends a couple of campsites down. Having used all my strength to get there, I collapsed in my friend's arms. Very quickly after that I began to lose all feeling in my body. First my fingers went numb and then my arms. The next thing I knew I couldn't feel my legs. Even my brain began to feel numb. I was losing my sight and my ability to talk or respond in any way.

Thankfully, my friends did all the right things. They laid me down near the fire, covered me with a warm blanket, and called 911. When the ambulance came, I was whisked off to the nearest emergency room where I spent the next two days unable to move as paralysis took over my entire body.

Miraculously, a doctor came into my path who was able to do the necessary surgery to reverse the paralysis I was experiencing. Because of that doctor, I am able to move and walk today. During my stay in the hospital, I was told by the doctors that my x-rays revealed a congenital spinal disorder, which had caused five of the seven vertebrae in the top of my neck to become fused together before I was born. When I fell, I slipped a disk in one of the remaining good vertebrae, and it was pressing on my spine.

I certainly appreciated the significance of my injury, and, just like my hospitalization after my first fall, I knew I would have to endure a long recovery period. However, my mindset, was different and *that* made all the difference in the world. Today, no matter what comes my way, I'm ready to *LEARN*.

Following that first operation on my neck, the surgeon informed me I would likely need a second surgery within a two-year period. While I could have allowed myself to worry about when and if that would happen, I decided instead to get on with my life. In the five years that elapsed before I did finally need the surgery, my wife and I had two beautiful children whom I was able to play with and enjoy like any other father. For that I am truly grateful. Had I taken a different approach and become preoccupied with my neck, I know there is no way I could have enjoyed a normal life during those five years. It would have been lost time to me (and my family) forever.

> *Life is about learning and growing*
> *each and every day!*

Despite the surgeries and other challenges I have faced, nothing that has happened to me has convinced me to stop making the most of the opportunities that come my way. Today, my wife, Cheryl, and I continue to watch our two beautiful daughters grow. We recently opened our own law office in Kamloops. I also continue to accept as many speaking engagements as I can fit into my schedule and am involved in a few other business ventures that I am very optimistic about. Most important of all, I know that all of the experiences that have come my way have helped me to learn and grow into a stronger, more capable person.

> *Life is meant to be lived moment to moment!*

Two times in my life, so far, I should have died—yet I didn't. Both times, like Lazarus, I was given the gift of another chance at life. What I've learned as a result is just how important it is to make the most of every moment I've been given. Challenges may come and unforeseen events will undoubtedly happen, but I'm too busy *L*iving *E*very *A*spect of my life *R*ight *N*ow to worry about the things I can't control. I hope you are too.

Promise to *LEARN*: *L*ive *E*very *A*spect of Your Life *R*ight *N*ow

This present moment is all we are promised. There is no past or future. There is only the now. Live for today and make the most of this moment.

A number of years ago as I was preparing to talk to an audience about what it means to *L*ive *E*very *A*spect of your life *R*ight *N*ow (*LEARN*), I decided to begin by telling a story that I once heard. It is the story of a little boy who wanted to play with his father. The father had promised to play with the son when he had time. As you can imagine, the father was a very busy man—working all day long, trying to pay the mortgage and other bills, wanting to give his kids all the things he hadn't had growing up. You know, the usual things that we adults spend our time doing.

One day after work, the father was sitting at home reading the newspaper when his young son asked him to play as he had promised. But the father was tired, so he tried to think of some way to put the boy off. Looking at his paper, he noticed a big picture depicting a map of the world and got an idea. Ripping out the page, he continued to tear the map into small pieces and then handed the pieces to his son.

"Take these," he said, "and once you've put the pieces back together, I'll be ready to play."

As the boy went off with the torn pieces of the map, the father sat back in his favorite chair, confident that he now had all the time in the world to relax. To his surprise, five minutes later the little boy was back with the picture from the newspaper now taped back together. Seeing that every piece of the map was in its proper place, the father looked at his son in utter amazement. I mean he was absolutely flabbergasted.

"How did you do that?" asked the father. "How did you do that so quickly?"

The little boy innocently looked up at his father, not knowing why he should be so surprised. "Daddy," he said, "On the front of the page you gave me was the map of the world. But on the other side was a picture of a boy. So I just put the little boy back together, and when I turned the page over, the world was all together too!"

We all have the pieces to our own puzzles!

Life is like a puzzle, I believe, and every one of us is born with all the pieces of our own puzzle intact. Unfortunately, the process of living can scramble the pieces and cause us to become confused. Our task then is to put the pieces back together in a way that makes sense to us. While each event in our life represents another part of the puzzle, it is up to us to determine the significance of specific events and how they fit together with other pieces. We ask ourselves about the puzzle pieces: Will they be the focus of the picture or just part of the background? The meaning that we attach to each event, each piece, is dependent on what kind of picture we want to create. Living *E*very *A*spect of our life *R*ight *N*ow (*LEARN*) helps us to figure out how those pieces fit together.

Are you ready to LEARN?

Many of us spend a great deal of time and energy thinking about past problems and worrying about future concerns, not realizing that in doing so the present is passing us by. While we're busy agonizing about things we can't change, we're missing out on the opportunity to make the most of every moment and *LEARN*.

How do we get ready to *LEARN*? The first step is to practice living in the moment—being present, engaged, and ready to respond to whatever is going on around us right now. Rather than worrying about missed chances or past mistakes, make the most of the relationships and opportunities right in front of you. Instead of worrying about what could happen in the future, make a plan for what you want and start taking steps to make it happen right now. Living every aspect of your life right now helps you figure out how the pieces of your puzzle fit together.

It's okay if you don't have all the answers!

I don't know all the answers, but I do know that as long as I keep searching and putting my puzzle together, it's going to be all right. My belief in my ability to find the answers when I need them has certainly been reinforced by my experience as a parent.

Parenting is a difficult challenge. It's hard to prepare yourself before you actually have a child. When my first daughter, Brooklyn, was born, I spent a lot of time worrying if I was doing it right. Then I saw an interview with a young father who shared that he had experienced the very same worries I was feeling. He talked about how he had been able to overcome them. As he explained, shortly after he had his first child, he admitted to himself that he didn't know how to be a dad, so he just accepted that he would learn to be the dad his child needed him to be.

Listening to him talk about how his decision had set him free and allowed him to enjoy the process of learning alongside his child, I realized that my own daughter didn't need me to be the perfect dad either. What she needed was for me to love her and do my best to teach and guide her.

When my second daughter, Maxwell, came along, I found myself facing an entirely new worry. Having experienced emotions I had never felt before when Brooklyn was born, I was afraid I couldn't possibly love my second child as much as I loved my first. Overwhelmed by my love for my older daughter, I didn't know if there was room in my heart to love two children with the same intensity.

My fear was quickly put to rest shortly after meeting Maxwell for the first time. Although she was in the neonatal care unit, and I wasn't able to hold her, I could put my hands in and touch her. When I did, she grabbed onto my finger and wouldn't let go. Every time I tried to withdraw my finger, she would cry. For four hours, I stood next to her as she held onto my finger because I couldn't bear to make her cry. Seeing her tiny hand holding on so tightly, I was completely engaged in the moment, in the connection that I felt to this new person in my life.

I had no more doubts in my mind. My heart was more than big enough for my two girls.

> *When we are ready to LEARN, we will find the answers we need!*

When I was struggling to learn to read and write at the age of fifteen, if the tutor my benefactors had assigned to teach me had been completely traditional and structured in his approach, he would have failed because I wasn't able to respond to that approach (there had been nothing traditional or structured about my life in the ghetto). To his credit, when he saw that I was interested in the murder trial and incarceration of boxer Rubin ("Hurricane") Carter, my tutor exploited that interest to teach me. He took me to the library and showed me how to research and find resources that would give me more information, and then he used those materials to teach me to read and write. Because he was engaged in the moment and paying attention to what I needed from him, my tutor was able to be the teacher I needed him to be. Together, we were successful.

Being ready to *LEARN* applies to everyone:

- If you want to be the boss your employees need you to be, it applies.
- If you want to be the doctor your patients need you to be, it applies.
- If you want to be the teacher your students need you to be, it applies.
- If you want to be the partner your spouse needs you to be, it applies.

When we focus on what's important, we're ready to LEARN!

Sometimes life can be overwhelming. Finding a way to ground ourselves helps to keep things in perspective and filter out the noise that can distract us from living a life we find fulfilling. In my roles as a husband, father, lawyer, speaker, entrepreneur, and community volunteer, my life can get hectic. I set priorities and determine what I can do myself and what I need help with in the various areas of my life. This keeps me grounded and helps me to find the time to focus on what is important to me. Don't be fooled into thinking that you can, or need to, handle it all yourself. Giving up control in one area frees you up to have a greater impact in another area. It's up to you to decide what's most important.

Use your passion to LEARN!

To be the best "you" that you can be, it's necessary to take time now and then to reinvigorate yourself so you're in good shape to help others and be a role model—particularly for those who depend on you such as your children, spouse, and other family members. Although it might sound selfish, indulging in a passion that refreshes and replenishes your energy is an investment that pays huge dividends. Such activities can improve your overall health and your ability to handle the everyday stresses of life. For me, that passion is speaking to groups of people about my journey and the lessons I have learned along the way. Knowing that I can inspire others encourages me to continue to do my best.

Lack of motivation or enthusiasm is something that keeps a lot of people from doing things that would make their lives richer and happier—things such as getting involved in a community organization, learning a new skill that would advance their career, or helping others. There can be a lot of reasons for not feeling motivated, but they all have to do with our perception of how much control we have over our own lives. For a long time, I thought I was incapable of learning. Dwelling on that thought and the limitations I felt it placed on me sapped every ounce of energy I had.

Understanding what is holding you back and taking the time to sort out problems and resolve old issues will help you to move forward and fit a few more pieces of your puzzle into place.

Some people accept their lot in life!

An important part of being ready to *LEARN* is not just accepting the way things are if they aren't working for you. If you don't like the way your life is going, don't settle. Scramble the pieces and continue to look for a better way to fit them together. It's never too late to flip the coin and try something new. It's never too late to learn a few new tricks. You know that saying made commonplace by Robert Fulghum, "Everything I needed to know I learned in kindergarten." That's not exactly true. It can take a lifetime of practice to master the basic skills that were introduced to us in kindergarten, particularly the ones related to getting along with others. We've been duped into thinking that when school is over we're finished learning. There's always more to learn and explore. Commit yourself to being a lifelong learner, and you'll be ready to *LEARN* every day.

LEARN from the people you encounter!

We can learn a lot from the people we meet if we pay attention. Listening to people's stories and hearing what has worked for them is a great way to gather new ideas and viewpoints on the challenges in life. If I meet someone who has a particular perspective on something, and if I can see that that perspective works better than what I am doing right now, I won't hesitate to adopt that perspective for my own—likewise, I don't mind sharing what works for me if it can help someone else.

Make the most of your time, LEARN to engage!

In the first year of being a parent, I can honestly say I was overwhelmed and so was my wife. With speaking engagements across North America, I was traveling a lot. Cheryl ended up feeling as if she were a single parent. In coming to terms with the demands of my career and the needs of our family, together we realized that the most important thing wasn't always how much time I had to spend with our daughter, but what I did with that time. Since then, I have *LEARNED* to be fully engaged with my children and make the most of whatever time we have together. I've also *LEARNED* to apply this principle to every other aspect of my life. You can too.

3
Move Beyond the Circumstances in Your Life

No matter what challenges we face, it's vital that we make every effort to ensure that the circumstances we find ourselves in don't dampen our hope or limit the future we see for ourselves. But not allowing anything to hold us back is easier said than done. The biggest obstacle many of us face in changing our circumstances is not allowing ourselves the flexibility to make mistakes and still keep moving forward. If we recognize that more than one path can lead to success, we can allow ourselves to be more forgiving and open to take advantage of the opportunities and coincidences that happen every day. Trust yourself to do the right thing.

Don't let your mistakes define you!

Whatever decisions you made yesterday and wherever you find yourself in your life today, there's an opportunity to do things differently tomorrow. Just because your latest decision has you in a situation that seems negative, you don't have to stay there. If you have enough trust in yourself, you can take the lesson this experience has to offer and choose to move on.

> *Don't allow the things that the people around you*
> *say and do limit your growth!*

At the school I attended in Bed-Stuy, expectations weren't very high among the teachers about what the future would hold for their students. In all the time I attended, there were no lesson plans, no exercises on the blackboard, no homework, no structure, and basically no education. The only thing I could say we were learning was that we were not worth teaching.

On a typical day in most classes, kids were free to play cards and tic-tac-toe or talk with one another in low voices while the teacher sat at the front of the room reading a newspaper or magazine or occasionally going to the door to chat with one of the other teachers. Although there were books in the classroom for most subjects, they were kept at the back of the room. We were never instructed to go back and get them, so for the most part they were never used. A few bright kids in the class did go back to get books to read, but they were always careful not to draw attention to themselves and end up being targeted by a classroom bully.

At the end of each class, the bell would ring, and the students would disperse to their next class where a similar routine was in place. With no assignments and no tests, grades were dependent on attendance and how many times we had caused trouble in the classroom.

Having diligently attended school every day and with nothing to measure my performance except a report card that indicated I was standing third in my class, I assumed that once I graduated from high school I would be able to go on to college and pursue any career that I wanted. That is, until the day that Mrs. Franklin instructed the students in my tenth-grade class to come up to the front of the classroom one by one and announce what they wanted to do in the future. When it was my turn, I nervously walked up and stood by her desk, creasing and re-creasing a piece of paper in my hand. I looked out at the bored faces of my classmates (most of them weren't even listening) and announced boldly, "I'm gonna be an attorney."

Thinking that she would say something approving like she had with other students, I was surprised when Mrs. Franklin leaned toward me and said in a low voice, "You need to do something more realistic with your life, Lesra. Learn a trade. Be a garbage man, you know, do something with your hands."

Stung, I slowly walked back to my seat, dejected and embarrassed.

Mrs. Franklin's comment haunted me for many years afterward, particularly as I struggled to learn to read and write. During all that time, the same question kept going around and around in my head, *Was she right, was I too dumb for college?*

For most of us, both teachers and parents play an important role in guiding and shaping who we become. Unfortunately, they aren't always able to set the example we need them to, so we need to look elsewhere for inspiration. In my case, both my parents allowed the circumstances of their lives to get the best of them. Unable to face up to a disabling back injury and the fact that he could no longer hold down the job that had allowed him to provide for his family, my father turned to alcohol rather than looking for other options. As our financial circumstances worsened, and as we ended up moving to Bed-Stuy, my mother too began to drink and withdraw into her own world. On many nights, I recall being awakened by their loud arguments and fighting that eventually became physically abusive.

I stand on the shoulders of my mom and my dad, and I am able to see beyond what they could see because they have given me something to stand on.

I didn't want to repeat the mistakes that I watched my parents make as I was growing up. I was motivated to make different choices in my life and model myself after people like Grandma Costa and Sam, the bar owner, who represented the kind of life I wanted for myself. The painful experiences of my childhood taught me this: Even in the darkest part of your life, a valuable lesson can propel you forward.

> *The past can stop you. But it can also*
> *help you grow!*

Moving beyond your circumstances is all about taking stock of the resources at your disposal and not allowing your frustrations and resentments to take over—to appreciate what you have been provided. In my early twenties when I was attending a university for the first time, I would often find myself thinking, *if only I had parents who gave me as much as some of these parents have given to their kids: money, cars, summers at the cottage, the opportunity to travel and experience the world and so many other advantages.*

Later on I came to understand that I had my own set of advantages, such as the ability to deal with adversity and a deep inner strength that was the result of overcoming difficulties and facing challenges head on.

> *Build on your strengths and focus on the positives!*

When you're facing a hurdle or a roadblock, look to someone in your life who is an inspiration—somebody who has made the effort to encourage you or a person you look up to for their own accomplishments. Thinking about these people can assist you to move beyond your own situation and not be totally defined by your past. Life is a constant process of redefining.

> *Decide not to be an obstacle in your own life!*

Once you accept that your mind has the ability to throw up roadblocks, it helps you to change your focus and start working to eliminate the things that are hindering you. When you've faced challenges, you realize you can handle almost anything that life throws at you.

I want to share two stories that illustrate how even the most difficult circumstances can be overcome. They are both stories of people whose lives were hard. Both faced great adversity but also wanted a better life for themselves and were willing to do the work to make that happen. As a result, the best began to happen. Help and assistance came to them when they most needed it. Strangers invested in them, and the dividends far exceeded what anyone would ever have imagined. These stories are quintessential examples of what happens when we believe that we can move beyond where we are and build the life we truly deserve.

The first is the story of Elizabeth Murray, a young eighteen-year-old white girl from New York. In fact, she was from the neighborhood right beside mine. Elizabeth was faced with a difficult journey in life. Both of her parents were drug addicts who spent whatever money they came across on their habit. To say the least, Elizabeth and her sister were neglected and deprived of basic necessities such as food and warm clothing. By the time she reached the age of fifteen, young Elizabeth, along with her sister, found herself homeless following the death of her mother from AIDS. Caught up in his own addiction, her father had sunk into a life on the streets and was neither willing nor able to fulfill his responsibilities as a parent.

Despite the fact that she was homeless, Elizabeth was determined that she would not suffer the same fate as her parents. She decided that literacy and education were her only way out. She continued to go to school every day and applied herself, studying in stairwells or anywhere else she could find a bit of shelter. As a result she graduated without the school officials ever knowing that she had been homeless.

Elizabeth's hard work and determination paid off in other ways too. Shortly after graduation, she won a highly selective *New York Times* scholarship for needy students and gained acceptance into Harvard University. Imagine that, a homeless girl going on to attend Harvard. And you know something else? When her story was featured in the *New York Times* as one of the winners of the scholarship, a number of readers were so touched and moved by her determination that they donated an additional $200,000—enough for fifteen more scholarships. I tell you, there are good people in this world.

The other story I want to share is that of "The Man on the Train"—the story of Simon Alexander Haley. For this one, we have to go way back to the late 1800s and the early 1900s, a time when black and white people here in North America didn't get along very well.

Simon was born on a farm in Savannah, Tennessee. He was one of eight children. Of all the children, Simon was the one chosen by his mother to be educated off the farm. It took some doing, but his mother eventually convinced his father, who would have to do without the extra set of hands to help out.

When Simon had finished grade school and it was time to go off to college. Simon's father handed him $50, told him not to ask for any more, and sent him on his way. Simon used the money to enroll in an agricultural and technical college in Greensboro N.C. (you might know it as A&T). To his embarrassment, it wasn't long before poor Simon found that he was the laughing stock of the entire college because he had only one pair of pants and one pair of shoes.

Unfortunately, Simon couldn't do much to change the situation regarding his attire. He was already working numerous spare jobs just to keep himself at the college. He worked as a waiter, handyman, and also as a helper at a school for wayward boys. In addition, during the winter months he earned extra change by getting up at four in the morning to make the rounds of several prosperous homes nearby and get the fireplaces started so that the well-to-do residents could arise in warmth and comfort. Although his enterprising ways were helping to pay for college, Simon soon found that having so many odd jobs was beginning to take its toll. With little time for study and sleep, his grades dropped, he failed a course, and soon he realized that he might have to drop out altogether.

As luck would have it, that summer, fate intervened, and Simon was one of twenty-four young black college men selected to be sleeping car porters on a train. While he was on the job early one morning (it was about 2 a.m.) his porter's buzzer sounded, and he jumped from his bunk to attend to a distinguished elderly gentleman who was having difficulty sleeping. The gentleman requested some warm milk, and Simon was quick to respond.

When Simon returned with the milk, the man engaged him in conversation, asking Simon questions about himself despite the fact that the rules at the time strictly prohibited personal conversations between the porters and passengers. The man was especially interested in learning how Simon had become so well spoken. Simon explained that he was a student at A&T College, not revealing, of course, that he might have to drop out because of his financial situation.

After more conversation, the man wished him a good night, and Simon returned to his quarters. The next morning the man gave Simon a $5 tip for his service. At that time, fifty cents was considered a good tip, and $5 would have been considered extremely extravagant. Even more amazing, when Simon returned to college, he was quickly summoned by the headmaster who revealed that the man on the train had paid Simon's board, tuition, and books for the entire school year.

The man's name was Mr. Boyce, a retired executive of the Curtis Publishing Company. Because of the kindness of Mr. Boyce, Simon did not have to work odd jobs during the school year, and he no longer needed to get up at four in the morning during the winter months to earn extra change.

Simon went on to graduate first in his class, earning a full scholarship to Cornell University in New York. He also married and had several children, all of whom distinguished themselves academically. One of those children you have no doubt heard about. Here is how Alex Haley (author of *Roots*) concludes his story about *The Man on the Train*:

> *Mr. Boyce dropped like a blessing into my father's life. What some may see as a chance encounter, I see as the working of a mysterious power for good ... and I believe that each person blessed with success has an obligation to return part of that blessing. We must all live and act like the man on the train.*

Isn't that something? I doubt that Mr. Boyce had any idea how far reaching his gift would be in changing the future of the young porter he met on the train, but it illustrates the point that I made in chapter one that there are many good people in this world.

Education is a key that opens many doors!

As both of these stories demonstrate (and my story too), education is one important step that anyone can take to move beyond the circumstances in their life. Knowledge is power. Once gained, no one can take it away from you.

Promise to Move Beyond the Circumstances in Your Life

Stop thinking about what is happening to you and start thinking about what you can make happen.

There are times in all of our lives where we have to decide whether we are going to step up and take control or relinquish that power and let "someone" or "something" else decide our fate. In 1998, I faced exactly that dilemma as I stood on the threshold of realizing my dream.

Having made it through my undergraduate studies and graduated from law school, I was preparing to sit for my bar examinations. The dream I had had since childhood of becoming a lawyer was finally within my grasp. The end of the road was in sight. Nothing was in my way when, out of the blue, I suddenly stumbled. After all of the hurdles I had overcome to get an education and all of the trials that had brought me this far, I found myself face to face with a totally unexpected fear—the fear of closing the door on my past and opening a new door that would lead to my future.

After I had failed the same exam twice, I finally understood what was happening: I was stopping myself. Afraid of crossing the threshold that would signify my triumph over the past (a past where I was more likely to need a lawyer than become one), my mind was throwing up roadblocks, testing my will and determination to see if I really had the guts to drive right through. As a result of that struggle, I learned that the greatest obstacle between me and unlimited success *was* me! I also came to realize how much of a psychological and emotional hold the past still had on me. Knowing that, I was ready to take on my fear, get into the driver's seat, and chart my own course—and once I did, the future that opened up before me was as wide as the horizon.

Your circumstances can't define you unless you allow them to!

You know that old saying about how you don't get to choose the people in your family? Well, the same goes for circumstances. We don't get to choose a lot of what actually happens in our lives—where we're born and the circumstances of our upbringing, the illnesses that will affect our health, and the people who will come into our path. Thankfully, that's not the same as saying we don't have any control, because we do. We get to choose what we do about the things that happen in our life. We get to decide what we accept and what we reject. We get to determine how much importance we give to a certain situation, event, or person and how much we allow these things to influence our choices.

Life is full of surprises, ups and downs, twists and turns, starts and stops—the trick to dealing with these circumstances is to not take them personally. Good things and bad things happen to everyone. Don't let circumstances determine how you approach life or what you are capable of accomplishing.

It's up to *each one of us* to determine who *we* are, where *we* want to go, and how *we'll* get there. Don't let your circumstances define *you*. Only *you* can define *you*. If you don't like the circumstances you find yourself in, start looking for ways to keep moving until you find something better. We all have the power to change, and no matter how old we are, there's always something new to explore.

Learn from your past struggles and trust what you learn!

It's not unusual to get hung up on our past mistakes, second guessing the decisions we've made and running through the "shoulda, coulda, woulda's" over and over in our mind. What we need to remember is that mistakes are just life experiences, nothing more. Their purpose isn't to torment us but to help us realize when we are headed in the wrong direction or where we need to make adjustments to our plan. The next time you find yourself dwelling on a mistake, ask yourself, "What did I learn from that experience?" and then use that knowledge to take a step forward and move beyond the mistake.

Forgive yourself and others for not being perfect!

To really move beyond our circumstances and be happy, we have to be able to put the past to rest. A big part of that is forgiving the people who have hurt us or those we have blamed for our circumstances. The ability to come to terms with my parents and the way they brought me up—to accept that they weren't perfect, that they struggled with their own demons but still wanted the best for their children—provided me with a greater sense of release than I could have ever imagined. Accepting them for whom they really were and loving them anyway gave me the ability to move beyond much of the frustration and anger I had felt about their bringing our family to Bed-Stuy. The lessons they tried to instill in me gave me the potential to move beyond the circumstances in my life. The fact that they were willing to let me go, to give me a chance to be educated and have a better life provided me with the motivation to do them proud and make the most of the opportunity.

Holding onto past hurts (playing the part of the victim) and thinking you don't need to resolve them is like having a malignant tumor and deciding not to do anything about it. It eats away at you and interferes with your enjoyment of life. It also limits the potential you see for yourself. By forgiving and choosing to move on, we take the power that the situation (or person) once held over us and turn it into positive energy.

Don't sell yourself short by settling for less!

How do you feel about your life right now? Are you happy with your circumstances? A lot of people feel dissatisfied with their life, but they never do anything about it. They wait and hope that things will get better on their own or someone will rescue them. That rarely happens, and even when it does, if we're too busy complaining or having a pity party, it's unlikely we'll notice when that opportunity comes along. It is our responsibility to create the circumstances we want and to build a life worth living.

George Bernard Shaw said, "People are always blaming their circumstances for what they are. I don't believe in circumstances.

The people who get on in this world are the people who get up and look for the circumstances they want, and if they can't find them, make them."

Life is short—too short to spend it feeling trapped by circumstances. When you aren't happy with how your life is going, explore what is bothering you and use that information to make changes. Ask yourself, "What can I do today to get what I want in my life? What will I say no to? What will I say yes to?" Then take action. Promise yourself to move beyond the circumstances in your life.

4

Don't Miss Out on Opportunity:
How a Blind Lady Helped Me to See

As you go along your path in life, if you are lucky enough, you will be able to recognize when certain events happen that let you know in no uncertain terms who you really are and what you're really made of. Earlier, I mentioned someone I affectionately call Grandma Costa. The discovery of this eighty-two-year-old blind lady turned out to be just that kind of event in my life.

Looking back, when I think about our coming together, I realize why it's no wonder that she was one of the first people I thought about when I needed inspiration to fulfill my promise to begin focusing on the positive. The fact that she instinctively trusted me and had faith that I was capable of living up to that trust formed the basis for a major turning point in my life. She forever changed the way I viewed myself and the world around me. If I had had enough faith to pray for a miracle at that time in my life, I couldn't have asked for a better one than Grandma Costa, even if at first glance it didn't look that way.

Picture this, on one side of the equation you have a little old blind lady who trusts no one, living alone with a seeing-eye dog and steel gates on her doors. On the other side, there's me, a scrawny street urchin who hustles at the local grocery store to get enough money for food.

It sounds like a recipe for disaster.

At the time I met her, my life had taken a turn for the worse. I was packing groceries simply to earn nickels, dimes, and maybe even a quarter here or there, in the hopes that, by closing time each night, I'd be able to put my change together to equal a dollar or two. I would use the money to buy rice, beans, or whatever else I could afford that day for me and my brothers and sisters to fill our bellies and ease the ever-present hunger pains.

Every day I grappled with the hardships that had befallen my family, searching for answers but never finding any. I was drowning in a sea of anger, frustration, and fear. My life teetered precariously on the edge. It was only a matter of time before I wound up like so many other young men from the ghetto—in jail, strung out on drugs or dead, or killed in some meaningless gang fight. Meeting Grandma Costa freed me from the spiralling hopelessness that threatened to swallow my life.

It would have been easy to abuse Grandma Costa's trust. Given my circumstances, I could have felt perfectly justified in doing so. All around the neighborhood I could see people robbing and stealing to make ends meet, and I understood as well as anyone how being desperate and the simple need for necessities like food could override everything else.

That I didn't and that I couldn't take advantage of my relationship with Grandma Costa told me (and defined for me) who I was and maybe, even more so, who I wasn't. That we even crossed paths at all on that autumn day shortly after I had been released from the hospital after my fall from the building is sheer coincidence. A minute later and I would have been out the door of the A&P grocery store, heading down the street to hustle groceries at another store.

Because it was the weekend, a lot of kids stood outside the A&P that day, mostly making a nuisance of themselves, not really interested in making tips. In contrast, for me, earning tips by bagging groceries would make the difference between whether I would eat or go to bed hungry that night. To the store's manager, Roger, we were all the same, a nuisance, and he did his best to shoo us out the door. Luckily, not everyone viewed me as an annoyance. Dorothy, a big-hearted cashier who appreciated my skills at packing groceries, often let me stand beside her at the till.

"This is my boy, Larry," she'd tell customers. "He's a hard worker." Although she never got my name right, hearing the pride in her voice when she said it always made me stand a little straighter and work a little harder around Dorothy.

On this particular Saturday afternoon, I had already put in several hours next to Dorothy without earning a dime. People either mistook me for an employee or simply didn't need help carrying out their purchases. It was torture to be surrounded by food when I wasn't making any money. Driven by hunger and hoping I wouldn't get caught, I sometimes stole candy bars that had been stashed beneath the counter. Now, my belly growled as I stuffed fresh loaves of bread and packages of food into bags, thinking how lucky these people were that they could afford to buy even the basics.

The clank of shopping carts at the front of the store pulled me from my reverie. A small wisp of a woman, elderly and frail, was struggling to tug a cart free. Somehow, she managed to pull it loose and then deftly juggle the cart, her guide dog, and a white cane as she set off to do her shopping. Minutes later, I saw her again as I darted up an aisle to check a price for Dorothy. She was holding a can in trembling hands, and with her face mere inches from the label, she was examining it through thick eyeglasses and a magnifying glass.

Soon, traffic in the store died down. My pockets still empty, I considered my options for the day. Maybe I would have better luck down the street at another store. Suddenly I noticed Dorothy smiling, gesturing me over to her till. The elderly woman was waiting as Dorothy counted out her change.

Finally! Somebody who could use some help, I thought, hoping I'd earn a tip. I looked the woman over and decided there was no way in the world she could manage everything—half a dozen bags, the dog, and her cane.

"Can I carry your groceries?" I asked.

The woman hesitated peering into my face and scrutinizing my features. "That would be nice," she said finally. Hearing her response, Dorothy's eyebrows arched in surprise, but she said nothing as we headed off.

Although she lived only a block and a half from the store, Mrs. Costa generally took a taxi home to avoid the gang members who prowled the streets looking for their next victim. But I wasn't thinking about that as I pushed the door open with the shopping cart full of groceries. I was going to be able to buy food today after all.

As we slowly made our way down the street, I'm sure we looked an unlikely pair, both somewhat fragile and vulnerable: me, a raggedy-looking, skinny kid, still sore and limping from my injuries, and Mrs. Costa, a fragile, nearly blind old woman who barely came up to my chin. It suddenly dawned on me that getting her home safely rested entirely in my hands, so I was relieved when we stopped in front of her brownstone on Stuyvesant Avenue.

One of Brooklyn's fine old Victorian mansions, her home was stately, ornate, and damn near bulletproof. As we walked through the heavy wrought-iron security gates and entered on the lower floor where she lived, I looked around in wonder at the big windows, high ceilings, gleaming hardwood floors, and the beautiful mouldings and fireplaces from another era. Although bars covered every single window and door, I had never seen such a beautiful home.

Drinking in the surroundings, I set her packages down and waited for my tip. She took a bill from her purse and studied it closely before handing it to me. Despite the fact that I had seen her look at it carefully, when I realized she had handed me a ten dollar bill, I was sure she had made a mistake and I told her so.

A sign of trust was placed on my path.

"Oh son, I meant to give you a dollar," she said, genuinely surprised as I handed the bill back to her. She reached back into her purse and pulled out a small wad of bills that she spread on her upturned palm. It was the most money I had seen in a long time.

"Take a few dollars for your troubles?" she offered. I gently tugged three singles out, thanked her and left.

Back at the store, a huge smile spread across Dorothy's face. Eventually, Dorothy said, "Mrs. Costa has been coming in here for years, and in all that time she's never let anyone carry her parcels, and she never walks home. As long as I can remember, she's always taken a taxi to and from the store!"

I was perplexed.

As I continued bagging groceries until closing, my mind was filled with questions. *Why did Mrs. Costa let me help her? Why had she even bothered with me? Was it that she could hear the desperation in my voice and sense my vulnerability?* Something about me (although I don't know what it was) must have told her all she needed to know about me, because she had taken the enormous risk of letting me walk her home. I couldn't get the thought that she had trusted me out of my mind. How had she known that when she held out all that money that I wouldn't snatch it and run?

After that, I carried Mrs. Costa's groceries home once a week, usually on Saturdays, and I relished the time we spent talking together. Although I knew practically nothing about her life, her calm assurance and quiet courage in walking down those streets with me made me marvel at her strength. With only a minimum amount of sight and a tremor in her step, I thought she was incredibly brave to venture out in what I perceived to be such a helpless state.

About a month after our first meeting, Mrs. Costa suddenly stopped coming to the store. After no one had seen her for two weeks in a row, I imagined the worst and hurried over to her house to check on her.

"It's Larry!" I shouted, reaching through the iron gate to knock on her door. I could see Mrs. Costa's tiny frame as she hesitated behind the thick glass door, her face filled with indecision. *Did she even remember me?* I wondered. Or did she think I was some little street thug trying to trick her into opening the door?

"Come in," she called at last, and I watched as her worn fingers worked the lock on the iron gate.

"I haven't seen you for a while. Do you need anything from the store?" I asked.

"I've been sick for the past few weeks," she replied in a thin, trembling voice. "I was too tired to go to the store."

How long had she gone without food? I wondered, scanning her kitchen table, which was covered in store flyers and cut-out coupons. Relieved that she appeared okay, I followed her directions and looked for the items she had selected for her grocery order. Her hands hovered over the newspaper, shaking uncontrollably. She didn't seem to mind when I gently closed my hand over hers to steady them.

Realizing that she needed me as much as I needed her, I visited Mrs. Costa several times a week after that. As we slowly eased into a friendship, she patiently answered my questions and listened as I rambled on with my thoughts and ideas. I wanted to hear her explanation for the world around us. In my world, trust was a matter of life and death. How did she know who she could believe in? More importantly, why had she trusted me? How did she know (how could she be so sure) that I would never do anything to hurt her?

Sometimes kindness has a way of coming into your life when you least expect it.

Spending time with Mrs. Costa was like stepping into an alternate universe for me. I knew I was still in the neighborhood, but the rules of the street didn't apply here. I felt safe from the outside world when I was there in the brownstone, and a spark of hope began to grow inside me that perhaps my life wouldn't always be as bad as it had been since we moved to Bed-Stuy.

During my visits, I'd often slide into a chair at her kitchen table while she fried me a hamburger patty. We'd talk about all sorts of things. Mrs. Costa was always trying to feed me. It seemed to make her happy to watch me hungrily wolf down the food she offered.

She reminds me of Granny, I decided, thinking about my own Grandma Mabel from my mother's side of the family.

"You remind me of my Granny, is it alright with you if I call you Grandma Costa?" I asked, explaining how we would often catch the bus over to Granny's apartment on Fulton Street on Sunday for a visit and how Granny gave me apples and nuts whenever I went to see her.

"Well I am old enough to be your grandmother," she replied. It was all the answer I needed.

Soon, Grandma Costa began finding odd jobs for me to do around the brownstone, polishing the beautiful spindles on her stairs, scrubbing bathrooms, sweeping and then waxing the hardwood floors with her big waxing machine. I often wondered if she was finding things for me to do simply because she knew how much I needed the money. Even if she was, I was so grateful to be there that I wouldn't have wanted her to stop. Still, there were times when I would turn down her offers of payment or leave odd jobs undone just so that I'd have an excuse to come back the next day. It was enough for me to share her company and enjoy the sanctuary of the brownstone.

Allowed to roam freely throughout all four storeys, I used to get lost exploring. I loved to wander the hallways, peeking into rooms filled with old wind-up clocks, ancient stereos, and ornate antique furniture. In the basement I discovered piles of chairs next to a huge bar with stacks and stacks of thick 78 rpm records covered in dust. I pictured Grandma Costa leading a glamorous life in smoky rooms filled with friends, music, and laughter. Everything about the brownstone hinted at a more graceful, elegant time, something quite different from the mean streets that lay just outside the door now.

As we grew ever closer, I began to see Grandma Costa as a kind of guardian angel, sent to give me hope. For her part, I think she knew instinctively that I needed someone to watch over me. She expressed her concern about my education.

"Aren't they teaching you how to sound things out in school, how to spell?" she'd ask, frustrated to see that I had difficulty reading even the simplest words. She was bewildered when I thought olive oil was some kind of medicine. I could tell that my speech bothered her too.

"Coffee," she gently corrected after hearing my mangled "corfee." I also remember how it concerned her that I didn't have a phone where she could reach me.

"I need some way to get in touch with you," she insisted, so I gave her Granny's phone number. After that, she'd call me at my Granny's apartment on Sundays, and the two women started to chat regularly, becoming good friends. They shared a special bond, a connection to a past world I knew nothing about.

For my part, I was intensely curious to know how someone as gentle and kind as Grandma Costa would choose to continue to live in this neighborhood. Although she rarely talked about herself, eventually I learned that Grandma Costa was from the island of Nevis in the Caribbean. Born in 1896, she came to New York when her father's sugar cane crops failed and the family lost its plantation. She married a Jamaican man, and they had two daughters. In 1931, Grandma Costa and her husband bought the brownstone for $9,000— a small fortune for a postal worker and a seamstress.

The neighborhood, known as Stuyvesant Heights at that time, was a prosperous, middle-class community populated with different races and nationalities. Grandma Costa's next-door neighbors were German. Well-to-do blacks—doctors, lawyers, and dentists—owned brownstones in nearby neighborhoods. It was a time when kids could safely sit on their stoops long after dark, and the local beat cop would stop by for a friendly visit. At dusk, he'd rap his billy stick on the lamppost to let the kids know it was time to go home.

Grandma Costa earned her living standing at an ironing board, pressing and folding handkerchiefs all day long and then taking care not to wrinkle them as she painstakingly pinned them to cardboard squares. Later she got a job at F. Klein, a secondhand store on the square. She barely made any money, but whatever extra she did have was spent on her family or others, not on herself. That was Grandma Costa's life—years of manual labor, scrimping and saving to look after her family. The glamorous, grand parties of my imagination were just that. Although I did learn that Grandma Costa and her family would have friends over for dancing and music in the basement bar.

Grandma Costa stayed the same, but gradually the neighborhood changed around her. Waves of rural Southern blacks and West Indians moved into that part of Brooklyn during the forties, fifties, and sixties. Whites left for the suburbs, and more blacks began to rent and buy in the area. It was one of the few places in the city where they could buy homes. In time, the area now known as Bedford-Stuyvesant became one of New York's largest black communities. Rapid growth and overcrowding led to the gradual deterioration of neighborhoods, creating pockets of poverty amidst the elegant brownstones.

My Granny was one of those who had arrived in that great migration of job seekers from the South. Leaving behind five young children in West Virginia, she came to work as a domestic for a white family in Brooklyn. Like Grandma Costa, she worked long exhausting hours only to pocket $20 a month for her efforts. The wife of the family was cold and distant, demanding that Granny keep the house impossibly clean. One morning Granny finished washing the breakfast dishes, then came down the stairs with her packed suitcase. The woman begged and pleaded with Granny to stay. Needing the money for her own family, Granny managed to stick it out for another miserable year, storing cans of food under her bed until she thought she had enough to feed her kids back home. She longed to have the father of her children join her, but he died before he could make it to New York. A year after she returned to West Virginia, Granny packed up her five children and moved back to Brooklyn.

My mother was the youngest, only three or four years old when Granny returned to Brooklyn. There, not far from Grandma Costa's brownstone, my Granny had found a spacious apartment on Fulton Street that rented for $26 a month, far beyond her means. But Granny wanted that apartment, and she was determined to have it.

"You never know unless you try," she liked to say, living her entire life by that motto. She managed to afford the apartment by cleaning homes for her neighbors, barely scratching out a living at fifty cents an hour. And just like Grandma Costa, she fretted and worried, working hard to make a better life for her family. Granny never had much in her life, but she found a way to stretch a dollar and make the most of what was available. She brought us secondhand clothes that had been passed on from families in her neighborhood, handmade quilts, and stuff she knitted; she always did whatever she could to help us and protect us.

I guess I shouldn't have been surprised that Granny and Grandma Costa were alike in many ways. They shared a common history, a time when New York was a very different place. I began to see how each of these women had been able to make a better life for herself in a new place despite whatever hardships or difficulties she faced because each had the heart to believe that she could do it. I also realized how much grandmothers provide a deep, enduring connection from one generation to the next, how they are the glue that binds families together. They give us direction, shape our identity, and remind us of the strength we carry inside.

Over the next two years, Grandma Costa became a big part of my life. When I left for Toronto, I took with me the important lessons she taught me through her kindness. Thanks to Grandma Costa, I now understood that the circumstances of life don't have to define you. I also knew that I could be trusted, that it was okay to feel compassion, and that I could assist others even though I might not realize I had something to give. Grandma Costa saw in me what perhaps I didn't see in myself. She took me into her home and openly shared all she had without fear that I would take advantage. She made it possible for me to buy food for my family at a time when it was desperately needed. Grandma Costa's kindness reached through the shadows of despair in my life. She treated me as if I were someone special. And whether she knew it or not, she kept me from turning down the same path that my brother Fru had taken. She was like a life ring, tossed to me in a deep, vast ocean.

"It's important to have dreams," she often told me. "To travel to new places, do new things and meet new people." I've never forgotten that advice.

Grandma Costa showed me the potential inside of myself.

Although some things about Grandma Costa remained a mystery to me, it wasn't hard to recognize her decency and to see her old-fashioned civility and sentimentality. I think she understood far more than I ever imagined, and I'm thankful that she had the clarity of sight to see something worth nurturing in me and to help me see it too.

Grandma Costa gave me the courage to believe in myself.

Before I met Grandma Costa, with little in life to compare my experiences to, I couldn't imagine what life was like outside my grim environment. Grandma Costa brought light and hope to my life. If it hadn't been for her taking me under her wing, I'm not sure how I would have survived those years in Bed-Stuy. Were it not for Grandma Costa letting me know that I could believe in myself, I'm absolutely sure I would not have been able to take advantage of the opportunity to get an education when it was presented to me.

Today, whenever I think of Grandma Costa, I am reminded of the song "Amazing Grace." Grandma Costa brought grace into my life, and despite the fact that she was blind, she could see much more than most people. This blind woman helped me to see.

Promise to Embrace the Opportunities That Come Your Way

In the midst of difficulty lies opportunity; seize it and make it your own.

Many people feel they are entitled to things, that opportunities should be presented to them, not realizing that it is their duty to actively pursue opportunity for themselves. With every bit of luck, there is also the necessity for hard work and commitment to make something of it.

If you want to move forward in your life, look for opportunities!

Life is full of opportunity if we allow ourselves to welcome it. Opportunity exists in chance encounters with new people (I bumped into my benefactors while I was working at a summer job). Put yourself in new situations or respond to the people who reach out to you (Grandma Costa could have stayed behind her locked door, but both of our lives would have been poorer as a result). New ideas and direction come to us each and every day from many different sources. The reason we don't recognize or seize many of the opportunities they represent is because we get too caught up in the everyday shuffle to really pay attention. Rather than consuming life, life ends up consuming us.

If you want more out of your life, if you want to move forward, experience more and grab the potential that's just waiting for you, start looking for opportunities. Look for opportunities in the meetings you attend (how can you help others, what new projects would you love to collaborate on?), in your telephone conversations (do you really listen to what others have to say?), even when you're waiting for the elevator or bus (how often do you strike up a conversation with a total stranger?). Be on the lookout for new ideas all around you. Be a student of opportunity—keep your mind open and aware. Listen to new ideas, ask for more input, welcome feedback from others. Consciously look for opportunity in all interactions.

Opportunities have a way of presenting themselves as problems!

Whether we want them to or not, our lives are constantly changing. Some of the changes we embrace and others we see as problems. We need to remind ourselves that within every problem lies the seed of opportunity.

The challenges we face in life and the mistakes we have made are also opportunities in disguise. As uncomfortable as they can be, both force us to make choices, reinforce our values, see things in a new way, and expand our way of thinking.

Sometimes the most challenging and difficult events can have incredibly positive results in the long term (a heart attack can be a wake-up call to make changes, or the loss of a job can lead to a new and better career opportunity), even if we don't see it at the time. If you want to become more conscious of how you can turn challenges into opportunities, the next time you're faced with a problem, ask yourself the following questions to help you understand where the opportunity is:

- What am I being challenged to learn or change in my life?
- What place of comfort and familiarity am I being asked to leave?
- What point of view would I have to hold to see the opportunity in this situation?
- What do I stand to lose if I let this opportunity pass me by?

Some people have all the luck!

We've all met people who seem to have it all: natural talent, a great career, wonderful family, good friends, a prosperous lifestyle. Our first thought when we look at them is this: *Some people have all the luck. I'm sure they had advantages that I didn't.* I've even had people tell me this about my own life. Really! What they don't seem to understand is that there's a big difference between being lucky and taking advantage of opportunity.

If you look closely, I think you'll find that most of us so-called lucky people have a lot in common: We take chances, work hard, and look for ways to turn setbacks into advantages. In short, we make our own breaks. And you can too.

Opportunities don't always come with gift wrapping!

Opportunities aren't generally as obvious as we would want them to be. They don't knock on the door, send a formal invitation in the mail, or come with a pretty bow on top. Most of them are subtle. So how will we recognize them when they arrive? By understanding that there is opportunity in every situation that requires us to learn, grow, or move outside the parameters we have set for ourselves. When we let go of our preconceptions and set aside our rules, definitions, and expectations of opportunity, we open ourselves to finding the opportunity in every situation and around every corner.

To embrace opportunity, you'll have to push your fear aside!

Opportunity offers us a chance to be more than we ever believed we could and to do things we never would have dreamed possible. But there's a catch. In order to make it happen, we have to overcome our fear. To embrace the life that could exist for us, we have to step away from what is comfortable and familiar. To accomplish more than we ever thought we were capable of, we have to open our minds to the possibilities and leave our self-imposed limitations behind. To embrace the person we have the potential to become, we need to acknowledge our fear and then push it aside and take the chances that are offered to us.

Prepare to be in the right place at the right time!

Often, people who appear to simply be in the right place at the right time have, in fact, worked hard to keep themselves open to the opportunities that come their way. They aren't afraid to talk to strangers, reach out to help someone else just because they can, or accept a challenge that takes them outside their comfort zone. They are the people who embrace life's possibilities with a "you never know where it might take me" attitude. If you want to get ready to be in the right place at the right time, you can start by saying yes to more of the things that come your way and make a promise to embrace opportunity.

5

What Mama Said: Timeless Life Lessons I Learned from My Mother

All parents try in one way or another to pass on the wisdom they have gained from their experience to their children. In my mother's case, those lessons came in the form of little expressions that peppered her everyday speech such as, "Don't spend it all in one place" or "You learn something new every day."

Although I wasn't always able to appreciate what my mother was trying to instill in me as a child, today her common sense expressions inspire and guide me as I teach my own children. They also remind me of the hard times my mother faced and how, despite fighting her own demons, she did what she thought was best to help us survive in a harsh environment.

As I have said earlier, the worst of those times started when we moved to Bed-Stuy where my mother changed so much I hardly recognized her anymore. She lost her youth and her ability to be playful and smile. She also started to drink a lot more.

In contrast, I remember our life in Queens as some of the happiest times of my childhood. I believe my family was happy there too. We lived in a house on a well-kept street, and although there wasn't a lawn in our backyard, we had a basketball court instead. As kids we spent most of our time playing outside.

I remember too that my parents were certainly different people when we lived in Queens, especially Mommy. She enjoyed standing with us out on the sidewalk, turning the rope while we jumped double Dutch. Sweeping me up into her arms, she'd plant a kiss on my face or tickle me to coax out my blues when I was sad. She also hummed little lullabies and songs like, *"Put another nickel in, in the nickelodeon. All I want is loving you and music, music, music."*

Her singing was always the surest sign that Mommy was happy. She'd lock onto a high note and sing her heart out while she cooked and cleaned with the stereo blasting in the background. Mommy had a beautiful voice, like Billy Holiday—raspy, yet sweet, deep and soothing. Besides her singing, I remember how she loved to walk in the rain. She treated the rain as if it were a special gift meant just for her. She'd grab one of us kids and pull us outside to enjoy the downpour. Eventually, we learned to scatter as soon as we heard the big, fat drops start to splash down. I hated the rain, but somehow I usually ended up going with her anyway, hoping we'd take a quick trip around the block. But that was never the case. It was usually four or five trips before she was ready to fold up the umbrella and go back inside.

When I was young, I remember how strikingly beautiful Mommy was with her glossy black hair smoothed into soft curls pinned at the crown—her skin, a lovely milk chocolate, unblemished, with dimples on either cheek when she smiled. In those early years in Queens, her eyes were sparkling and full of life, but that was before eight kids, unpaid bills, booze, and too many hardships.

Another day, another dollar—Mommy always said that if you don't put in the effort, at the end of the day you aren't going to be any further ahead. Sometimes hard work is the only way to get what you want.

Even after Pop injured his back and our financial troubles began, Mommy still managed to look for the best in the situation. Swallowing her pride, she endured the deeply personal and sometimes insulting questions asked by the lady at the welfare office in order to get money and food stamps to keep us going. At the age of eleven, I began hanging out in front of the local grocery store offering to help people

53

with their bags for tips to buy food to help feed the family. Despite the fact that she must have been ashamed and embarrassed about what I was doing, she told me how proud she was.

"You're my little man," she said. "Right now, I don't know what I'd do without you."

> *Save the bones for Mrs. Jones, 'cause she sure ain't got no teeth. Mommy taught us that there's value in everything, so don't waste what you have. It was a lesson that had far too much relevance to our life in Bed-Stuy where we were lucky to get rice and beans for dinner and where meat became a luxury. Seeing the effect our new life had on my mother made me angry at the world.*

From the first moment we set foot in Bed-Stuy, everything changed. The expression on my mother's face changed, and the gentle, caring side of her seemed to vanish. Instead of the warmth and comfort I was used to, she became cold and aloof with me. I was hurt by her apparent indifference. Something had taken hold of her, something I couldn't understand.

Instead of showering me with her usual affectionate hugs, she'd push me away.

In Bed-Stuy, it seemed as if my mother's whole world shrank to become just the window overlooking the street. She'd lean on the windowsill for hours on end, her chin resting in her hand. Barely uttering a word, she watched life pass by, far removed from the rest of us. When she did speak, her comments were usually aimed at hardening us up to face the harsh realities she knew lay just beyond the window where she spent so much time.

One Sunday, I simply wanted to see her smile again. (She tended not to drink as much on Sundays, so she was sort of in that withdrawal stage after drinking heavily on Friday and Saturday. I knew she was struggling with the effects of it.) I asked if she wanted to go for a walk. It was raining outside, so I thought it might cheer her up, but she just looked at me vacantly and said, "No, no, I'm fine," and continued to putter around the apartment looking sad. She was never a melancholy person, but she became that way in Bed-Stuy.

Because I said so. With no satisfactory explanation from her as to why it was happening, I struggled to understand the change in Mommy's behavior toward me and took it as a sign that she no longer loved me.

I resented the person my mother became in Bed-Stuy, and I hated her constant pushing to try to toughen me up. "You're gonna have to learn to stand up on your own," she chided, her tone harsh and impatient. It was as if she had lost all hope in the possibility of a better future for us. She turned her back to me, and, suddenly, I felt as if I had become invisible.

I didn't catch another glimpse of the mother I had known and loved until I came to in the hospital after my fall from the building. Yet it wouldn't be until many years later when I was living in Toronto and preparing to go to the university that I would finally realize that she did indeed still love me. In fact, she had never stopped loving me. This realization (not long before her death from cancer) would eventually help me come to terms with the way she had raised me during those hard years in the ghetto and allow me to finally understand just how much she had sacrificed when she let me go.

Going back to my time in the hospital after my fall, I remember waking up one evening to the sound of someone crying softly. I turned my head as much as I could and realized it was Mommy sitting in a chair next to my bed.

"Oh my baby," she whispered as her soft, warm hand reached out and touched mine. "I was so scared you'd never wake up. You're gonna to be okay, I'm here."

I could see she was trying to be brave on my behalf. I can only guess what she must have been thinking at the sight of the tubes that snaked out of my nose, mouth, abdomen, and even my private parts (in addition to two fractured ankles and a broken wrist, I also had extensive damage to my kidneys and other internal organs). As she sat there, tears spilled down her cheeks. I could see a mixture of guilt and pain reflected in her eyes. Sensing that she blamed herself for my fall and seeing her in pain made me want to reach out to her and tell her that everything was going to be okay.

In the days that followed, I drifted in and out of consciousness, overwhelmed with pain and miserable during my waking hours.

Night after night, long after visiting hours ended, Mommy managed to get into the ICU. Sometimes she would appear at two or three in the morning and stand at the nurses' station, pleading to be let in. On those nights, she would sit in my darkened room, quietly crying, her face softened with concern.

"Don't try to talk," she'd say. "I just need to be here, to know that you're okay." Still hooked to tubes, I couldn't eat any solids, yet on every visit, my mother brought apples, fruit, and other luxuries that had long been absent from our lives. At home, we had been going hungry, our welfare money running out weeks before the next check was due. I wondered where she found the money to buy me these special treats.

Blood is thicker than water. Although I struggled to deal with my anger and frustration, the love Mommy showed during my time in the hospital pulled me through and gave me the strength to go on.

During those hours together at the hospital, Mommy would often lean over me to gently stroke my arm, and for the first time in months, I couldn't smell any booze on her. Her soft touch and her gentleness toward me were reassuring, but also confusing. In truth, I was deeply angry with both of my parents, blaming them for the mess of our lives. Along the way, an impenetrable wall had grown between my mother and me, built brick by brick upon the anger I felt toward her.

After more than five weeks of grueling, painful physical therapy, I awoke to the sound of Mommy singing one morning. The doctors had informed her that the worst of my injuries were healing. I was nearly ready to go home. Buoyed by the good news, she stood in the corner near the window, her voice raspy, shaky as she softly crooned the words to "I Can See Clearly Now," one of her favorite songs. It was the first time I had heard her sing since we left our home in Queens. She was acting like her old self, and I felt a glimmer of hope. Maybe she would find a way to love me again.

Hearing her sing created a deep ache in my heart. I was reminded of everything I thought I had lost in my mother: her vitality, her spark, and the passion she once held for life. I desperately longed to go back to Queens and back to the life we had before.

It didn't happen though. Upon my return home, Mommy slowly became quiet and withdrawn once again, defeated by circumstances, and I was forced to continue trying to find my own way in a world that I wanted nothing to do with.

Don't cry over spilled milk. Realizing that nothing had changed when I returned from the hospital, I allowed myself to get stuck dwelling on the past and what I'd lost.

Because of the wall between us and the resentment I had built up toward my parents over bringing us to Bed-Stuy, my real relationship with my mother didn't begin to develop until after I was taken away from that environment. I finally began to understand and come to terms with my mother during a visit home after I had spent several months in Toronto.

It was my first trip back in a long time. I had come into the apartment without her realizing I was there. As I walked through, I spotted my mother standing at the stove in the kitchen with her back to me. When I came up behind her to give her a hug, instead of being cool like I expected, she just kind of melted into me. It was one of the first times since I was very young that I could remember hugging my mother and her hugging me back. After a few moments, she turned to me and said with tears in her eyes, "I never knew that you loved me because for so long you wouldn't allow me to comfort you or even touch you."

People in hell want ice water. Mommy always said that it's foolish to spend time yearning for things you don't need or can't have. She also said that if you want for the wrong things or you go about getting them in the wrong way, you end up somewhere you don't want to be. This expression finally made me realize that I was missing out on the love that was behind everything she did for me. Instead, I was focusing on what I didn't have and wishing things had been different.

57

I struggled for many years with the way my mother brought me up during our time in Bed-Stuy because I didn't understand what she was doing. To me she seemed harsh, cold, and distant when all I really wanted was to be hugged, cared for, and loved. Looking back, I can see that I was a sensitive kid who didn't like to argue or fight (I just wanted everyone to get along). Having the benefit of experience, my mother saw that I was soft. She feared I wouldn't survive in the ghetto environment if she didn't harden me.

Years after I got out of Bed-Stuy, I started to make sense of how she had tried to protect me with lessons like, "Men don't cry" (which she reinforced by hitting me upside the head with a shoe). "You need to be tough, you need to be rugged," she would say. My response was to harden my heart not just against the world, but against her too. Although her lessons were appropriate to the circumstances, and despite knowing that what she did, she did for me, it still took me many years to get over some of the harsh lessons.

Now that she's gone and I have children of my own, I am grateful for the little sayings that Mommy passed down to me. Today, I am able to hold onto the good things, the lessons she shared with me, and to forgive the fact that she wasn't the mother I wanted her to be. Although I didn't understand her methods, I was eventually able to take some of the pearls of wisdom she had to offer. My mother never lived to see me realize my childhood dream of becoming a lawyer, but that doesn't really matter because I think she knew all along I had it in me. And that's why she wanted me to be strong and independent.

Here are more of my mother's favorite expressions. How many of them do you recognize from your own childhood?

- You will be judged by the company you keep.
- You can't get blood from a turnip.
- Ain't nothing to it but to do it.
- Mind your P's and Q's.
- I'll be back in two shakes of a lamb's tail.
- Never get too big for your britches.
- Keep your nose clean.
- Don't "hay" me. Hay is for horses. Moo is for cows.
- My nose is itching, company is coming.

- My ears are ringing, somebody is talking about me.
- Don't spend it all in one place.
- Save some for a rainy day.
- Do as I say, not as I do.
- There's always tomorrow.
- You learn something new every day.
- Sorry didn't do it, you did!

Promise to Use the Lessons That Life Provides

Gratefulness is the key to a happy life that we hold in our hands, because if we are not grateful, then no matter how much we have we will not be happy—because we will always want to have something else or something more.
David Steindl-Rast

When we are growing up, we often resist the lessons our parents are trying to teach us. Perhaps it's one of the few ways we can challenge their authority over us. Or maybe we need to learn some of those lessons firsthand. I'm not sure exactly, but whatever the reason, there comes a time in our life (usually when we've had the chance to make a few mistakes of our own) when it can be helpful to revisit some of those lessons and extract the nuggets of wisdom we couldn't see before.

In my case, although I may not agree with the method or approach my mother used in raising me, I've learned to understand and come to terms with our relationship enough to move forward and appreciate her role in my life. It doesn't mean that I adopt the same approach in my relationship with my own children, but rather that I understand she was doing the best she could under the circumstances and her intentions were good. The knowledge that my mother loved me and wanted the best for me helped to heal the hurt feelings I had carried for many years, and it also allowed me to accept the lessons she had to pass along.

Sometimes the lesson is what <u>not</u> to do!

My mother always told me, "Do as I say, not as I do." To me as a kid, that advice just sounded hypocritical. As an adult, I can understand that my mother never wanted any of her children to make the same mistakes she and my father had made. I learned a lot from the example of my parents and their inability to overcome their circumstances. For one thing, I realized that, in life, sometimes you need to know what you don't want to be in order to figure out what you do want to be. The experience of my parents also taught me that I needed to do something differently.

In Toronto, I found the circumstances I needed to build the kind of life I wanted for myself and the life I'm sure my parents would have wanted for me too. Even though they didn't provide the best role model for how to work through difficulties in life, I know my parents always tried to give each of their children what they believed they needed. Today I am thankful for that. In the end, the most important lesson I learned from my parents is that I need to interpret their role in my life in a way that lifts me up and helps me grow. I can't allow myself to be stuck in the past, dwelling on thoughts of what I missed out on or what my parents couldn't provide for me.

Value the wisdom of elders!

We can read all the books we want to try to figure out how best to live our lives, but some of the most valuable wisdom isn't found in books. It exists in the hearts and minds of our elders. Only one heart can teach another heart what the written word doesn't say. I often share that sentiment with my audiences because it summarizes nicely the role that elders play in our lives. With the unconditional love and support they offer, our elders teach us about the importance of being connected with one another. Through their stories, they also pass along important moral lessons and provide us with a living link to our ancestors and our history. Through their actions, they demonstrate important virtues that we need to cultivate in our own lives such as courage, faith, self-control, compassion, sincerity, empathy, patience, and reliability.

We must value the wisdom of our elders and recognize that they have a lot to offer us. Now at 102 years of age, my own Granny continues to share her knowledge and experience with all who are lucky enough to know her. Whenever we are in her presence, no matter what else may be going on at the time, every member of my family understands the importance of paying their respects to her.

We always have a choice!

Life is full of lessons. It's up to us to decide when we are ready to accept them. For example, when we are presented with a problem or obstacle, we can choose to learn the lesson that life is presenting, or we can ignore it and repeat the lesson later on. We can accept that adversity is part of life and look for the seed of opportunity that each difficulty represents, or we can allow it to make us angry and bitter. We can choose to seek happiness in our life, or we can decide to complain about things that have gone wrong. We always have a choice.

There is a difference between what we want and what we need!

The source of much of the dissatisfaction we experience in our lives is the unrealistic expectations we have set up for how things should be and what we need to live a good life. The more we want and believe we need, the more pressure we put on ourselves to chase after those things and ignore other priorities in our life. The more we see what other people have, the more we seem to think we need to have the same. But there is a big difference between what we want and what we need. Unfortunately, many of us don't learn this lesson until we lose what is really important to us and are left with the things we realize we no longer want.

If you're having difficulty determining the difference between wants and needs, simply ask yourself, "Does this opportunity/possession/situation that I am focusing my efforts on support the goals I've set for myself, or should I be focusing on something else that would better serve my needs?"

Passion is the fuel of success!

Passion has magical power. It can turn an ordinary person into an unstoppable force, dreams into reality, and resistance into support. When we have a passion for what we are doing, we are focused on our goals, not on ourselves. We get wrapped up in our dreams rather than in our worries, and we live in a place where there is no time for self-doubt or dwelling on what might have been. When we have passion, we no longer consider what we do as being work. When we encounter obstacles, we find a way around them and continue on our way until we reach our goal.

Enjoy the little things and be grateful!

One thing we instinctively know when we are children but seem to forget as we get older is that we should take time to enjoy the little things that make us happy. There is much joy to be had in the little moments that come and go every day—the joy of making someone smile, the joy of feeling the breeze brush past us, the joy of discovering something new. If we don't take the time to appreciate these little things and to be grateful for what we have, we deprive ourselves of a great deal of happiness that is literally ours for the taking.

Find your own meaning of life!

At some point along the way, nearly every one of us will get caught up in our own search for the meaning of life. But it is not the purpose of life to provide *us* with meaning. Quite the opposite. It is our purpose to *give* meaning to the life we have through the choices we make for ourselves and through the things we choose to give our attention to. What we *care about and what we care for become what really matters.* It's up to each one of us to decide what that will be. Promise to use the lessons that life provides to discover your purpose.

6

Let the Outside Reflect the Inside: Don't Be Afraid to Live Who You Really Are

I am invited to speak in front of groups of all kinds (from elementary school children to business executives). Each group looks for inspiration that can be applied in their own lives. I'm concerned about how preoccupied we've become with "motivational" programs that offer ten steps to being successful. In reality, how useful are these cookie-cutter plans in helping us to achieve what is most important in our lives and to really focus on reaching our own individual goals? My guess is, not very.

Unless you're talking about fun slide carpet skates, this "one size fits all" cookie-cutter approach rarely works. In terms of defining success, it's too confining. It doesn't encourage (or tolerate) originality, creativity, diversity, and flexibility, or explain all things that make the world a more interesting and enjoyable place to live. Success can't be defined in the same way for everybody, and I don't believe it should be because it sets us up for failure when we can't fit inside "the box."

My wife's brother, Paul, definitely didn't fit inside the box, yet he is a great example of someone who has found success by following his own path. You see, Paul is very artistic. At some point during his teen years, he started to get tattoos on different parts of his body as a way of expressing himself. As he got into his twenties, Paul had difficulty finding a job, and he felt that he wasn't successful because people always thought he was hiding something from them—and he was, himself. Whenever he went for a job interview, Paul would make himself presentable by putting on a tie, jacket, and dress shoes—clothes that he clearly wasn't comfortable in.

Tired of rejection and also of hiding the person he really is, Paul decided to take a different approach. He shaved his head, put on a pair of boots, and no longer tried to hide his tattoos. Almost immediately, he found a job working in the same industry where his passion laid and where people could appreciate his good qualities because he let who he is on the inside shine through to the outside. Today, Paul is the owner of a busy tattoo shop and art gallery in downtown Vancouver, living a successful life on his own terms.

> *Bring out your inner bling!*

Some people will tell you that success is measured by how much money you make or how much "bling" you've got, but the best bling of all is what you've got inside of you. It's whatever unique talent or gift you have to share with the world. If you want to be successful, you have to start thinking of yourself as a diamond in the rough and take the time to polish your skills. When you begin to embrace your inner bling, the bling comes out.

> *Real beauty isn't always visible to the eye!*

My benefactors in Toronto sparked my interest in learning and broadened my horizons by taking me to museums, art galleries, and cultural events. Being a teenager at the time, appearance was a big deal to me, and I had a well-defined idea of what I found attractive in the opposite sex.

On one such occasion, we were at a poetry reading. The first person on stage that night was the woman who had been taking the money at the door earlier in the evening. My first impression was that she was one of the plainest people I had ever seen in my life. However, when she took to the stage and started to present her poetry, it was all about beauty.

Sitting there, listening to her voice and the words she had written, I was moved so much that it began to change the way she looked to me. Suddenly, I looked at her in awe, riveted by her words. I realized she was gorgeous. That experience transformed my perception of beauty and caused me to start thinking about how I judged the people I came in contact with.

When we allow ourselves to be who we truly are, we attract the kind of people who can appreciate our qualities.

My first girlfriend in Toronto was a young English girl named Sophie whose well-to-do family owned an antique shop in the city. By all measures, she and I undoubtedly made an odd couple. Where her dress and overall demeanor were conservative, reserved, and very proper, I liked to wear flashy clothes. Because I was an American, I was far more demonstrative with my emotions. Although others may not have understood what drew us together, in addition to her classically British attributes, I found Sophie to be intelligent, engaging, and thoughtful, all qualities that were very attractive to me.

When I first met Sophie, I noticed she had the sweetest voice in the world—at least it sounded that way to me, in sharp contrast to my New York twang. Although we really were quite a pair, when I think about it, despite our obvious outward differences, we had a lot of similarities on the inside. I was very pensive, didn't make friends easily, and thought about things a lot—and so did she. As we got to know one another, Sophie and I spent more and more time together, hanging out, exploring the city, and talking about everything under the sun.

Although I felt a genuine connection with Sophie, for a long time I resisted dating her and becoming emotionally involved because I couldn't believe she found me interesting. In addition to my feelings of inferiority about growing up in the ghetto, I was shy about my body, not only because I was the only black kid in the neighborhood but also because I had high cheekbones that I was constantly trying to push in to make them look less prominent.

When Sophie made the bold move of inviting me to go to a cottage with several other young couples for a weekend, I was surprised. Not just that she liked me enough to introduce me to her circle of friends (whom I had never met) but also that by bringing me along she was essentially announcing to them that we were a couple. I was even more surprised when they arrived to pick me up in a big brown Cadillac with luxurious leather seats. The car belonged to the dad of one of the young men, and while he and his girlfriend sat in front, Sophie and I were alone together in the back. "What a world!" I thought as we headed to the cabin in luxury.

When we arrived at the cabin, Sophie's friends treated me as if I had been part of their group for years. As the girls went inside to unpack and make lemonade for everyone, we boys got busy chopping wood and taking care of other outside chores. Despite my color and my heavy New York accent, I never felt for a moment that anyone was judging me. This acceptance made me realize that the fears and insecurities I had about Sophie and me were just that, my own fears and insecurities.

In many ways, Sophie laid the groundwork for me to understand the difference between the outward and the inward aspects of ourselves. How someone appears on the outside doesn't necessarily match up with who they are on the inside. It takes time to get to know people. My deep connection with Sophie also set the standard in respect to my expectations for future relationships. In many ways I have her to thank for leading me to the woman who would become my wife.

Be generous. Share yourself with others!

My wife, Cheryl, is a very private person. When we first met at Dalhousie Law School in Halifax, Nova Scotia, we belonged to the same student association and occasionally spoke to one another at meetings. From those few brief conversations, it was clear to me that Cheryl was a bright, highly motivated person with a lot to offer the world, yet I noticed that she rarely took the time to interact with others. Every day just before class she would rollerblade in and find a seat in the lecture hall. Almost immediately after class, she would rollerblade out again without having spoken to a single person.

At the next association meeting I made a bold decision. I told Cheryl that I thought by rollerblading in and out every day she was depriving people in the school of the opportunity to benefit from knowing her. Not knowing if she would be offended or take my observation to heart, I was very happy the next day when I noticed she stopped in the vestibule and spoke with a few people after class, rather than strapping on her rollerblades and rolling away. For the two of us, it was the beginning of a friendship that eventually turned into much more. For Cheryl, many of the friends she made as a result of opening up and sharing herself while at Dalhousie are the same friends that she remains close to today.

> *We don't change people, but we can assist them by showing them a new path or opportunity!*

Interestingly, I think the development of that side of Cheryl's personality also became a critical element in her ability to deal with the very public demands of her life today—and the way she embraces and interacts with the people she meets. In the past I was the more outgoing partner in our relationship. Now I think she shakes far more hands and talks to many more people than I do, yet I doubt that she would be happy with the attention our life together has brought if she hadn't discovered the gifts she has to share with the world.

Promise to Let the Outside Reflect the Inside

You never find yourself until you face the truth. Pearl Bailey

We all have something special to offer the world, something unique to express and share—even if we haven't realized it yet. Many of the messages we receive starting from a young age lead us to believe that what is inside of us needs to be adjusted, toned down, censored, or adapted before we put it out there for others to see. "Don't say that," we're told. "You shouldn't feel that way," "You're just being silly," "Stop showing off." Do any of those sound familiar to you? As a result, we start holding back our real thoughts and feelings (disconnecting with our true self), wondering if we are normal, second-guessing "who" or "what" we really are. We also start to look to others for clues about how we should behave, and we begin to change who we are to conform to what is expected of us—and in doing so, we lose touch with what is unique and special about us.

Don't get me wrong, fitting in and getting along with others is important, but so is the ability to be who you were meant to be, not a carbon copy of someone else. We all have a responsibility to share who we are with the world. We also owe it to ourselves and others to share our gifts and talents. We deny others the opportunity to know us and benefit from what we have to offer when we hide who we are, minimize our talents, or pretend to be something we're not just to fit in with what society expects of us. We need to let our light shine through.

Take time to discover who you are!

We can't be ourselves and reflect who we are to others if we haven't taken the time to know, understand, and accept who we are first. Take the time to contemplate what you want most from your life. Imagine there is nothing to stop you. What would you do? Where would you choose to focus your time and energy? What kind of people would you surround yourself with? Where would you travel? What would you like to learn? What kind of lifestyle appeals to you? Try on different ideas and rediscover what excites you, what makes you tick (and what doesn't). Through trial and error, you can help define the person you want to be.

Be honest about who you are!

It's not easy to expose ourselves to the judgment of others, especially when we know that some part of who we are isn't going to be accepted or understood by everyone. The question we have to ask ourselves is this: Do we allow the prejudices of others to bully us or diminish who we are? And if we choose to hide that aspect of ourselves from view, how can we expect to connect with others who may need the support, understanding, or even leadership that we can offer? Only when we are brave and stand up are we able to convert prejudice into understanding. It is also important to give others the same amount of tolerance that we expect from them.

Be proud of your individuality!

We all feel self-conscious about certain traits because we think they don't measure up to our perception of what others have. We have to remember that these little quirks or differences are what set us apart from the crowd and give us a unique perspective on life. Instead of comparing ourselves to others, we should be showcasing what we have to offer. Whether it's something unique (even unusual) about the way we look, a natural talent (such as singing, athletic skills, or a way with numbers) that we were born with, or the way we express ourselves through our manner and style, we should be proud of what makes us irreplaceable.

It's not about being perfect!

Mistakes are a great opportunity for us to learn about ourselves. Accept that some things will work out better than you expected, and other things won't. Although people around you might raise their eyebrows or even be critical of your mistakes, as long as you can shrug and say, "Hey, I thought I'd give it a try" (and leave it at that), people will ultimately respect you for it, and you'll be that much further down the road to knowing yourself better.

Don't worry how others perceive you!

Worrying too much about what other people think of us can take a lot of the excitement and spontaneity out of life. It's also very difficult to be yourself when you're constantly wondering if you are being judged. Just accept the fact that you can't please everyone. Those who are worth your time will be easier to spot and more appreciative if you are being genuine and true to yourself.

Lighten up and cut yourself some slack!

We all make our fair share of social gaffes and experience uncomfortable moments from time to time; it's part of being human. So stop worrying and imagining the worst, particularly in social situations. Realize that every mistake you make is an opportunity for you to connect with others. Learn to laugh at yourself and the world will laugh *with* you, not *at* you. Turn your faux pas into funny stories that you can share with others; it lets them know that you don't think you're perfect and you don't expect them to be either. Everyone loves people who have the ability to laugh at themselves.

Believe in yourself!

As long as we're trying to be someone or something that we're not (or trying to live up to someone else's expectations), we deny ourselves the opportunity to be truly happy in life. We also don't realize how much energy it takes to hide who we are or how we feel until we let go of the pretence and experience the relief it brings. While we were living in the ghetto, my mother often worried that I was such a sensitive kid, so she tried everything she could think of to toughen me up (even hitting me with a shoe). In that environment, it wasn't safe to show vulnerability. I struggled with trying to act like a tough guy when I really wasn't. Today, I am happy that I can just be myself, to express my emotions, talk to the people I meet on the street, and smile whenever I feel like it (which turns out to be most of the time).

To be happy, we all need to be free to be ourselves and to show the world we're proud of the way we are—by trusting in our own judgments and opinions, by focusing on finding the direction that is right for us, by believing in ourselves, and, above all, by promising to let the outside reflect the inside.

7
Nothing Happens by Accident: Prepare Yourself to Take Advantage of Coincidence

When we are open to the possibilities and ready to embrace opportunity, it's amazing how easily things begin to happen in life as one coincidence after another comes along to help us move forward with our goals. When I gave up my fear and began to focus on the positive, accepting that I could learn, that I could make a contribution, that I could make a difference, it was as if I had simultaneously set in motion a series of miraculous events that continue to shape my life even today.

The first of those events was my discovery of Hurricane Carter's autobiography, *The 16th Round*. I found a tattered copy at a used book sale in Toronto. I paid twenty-five cents for that book. It was the first book I tried to read on my own. Can you imagine twenty-five cents changing your life? It changed mine.

As I was reaching down into the bin to get the book, a man standing beside me suddenly picked it up, glanced briefly at the back cover, and then walked away with it. Now picture this, there were thousands of books around me, but for some reason, I couldn't get that particular book off my mind, so I followed the man around for the entire time I was at the sale—about two hours.

I kept looking at the man with the book. He kept looking at me. I'm sure he must have been saying to himself, *Why the heck is this kid following me, what does he want?* Eventually, to my amazement, the man set the book down. I couldn't believe it. I hurried over and snatched it up. Thank goodness I still had my street reflexes.

Stumbling through that book changed my life. I needed to tell the author that he had reached me. His story had touched me and been the breakthrough I needed to overcome my illiteracy, so I wrote Rubin a letter. The miraculous part was that Rubin responded. After a few months of writing back and forth, I asked Rubin for permission to come to New Jersey to see him in person.

Rubin fired back his reply lickety-split saying, "No, absolutely not!" He was trying to get out of that place not bring people in there. Besides, he told me, he had not had a personal visit in over five years, and he wasn't about to change that now. But, as coincidence would have it yet again, I did not get that letter. At least, that's my story and I'm sticking to it.

I arrived at the prison. When the guard told Rubin he had a visitor, he knew it had to be me. Since I had traveled such a long way, he decided that he would see me this one time. That first meeting was an emotional one for both Rubin and me, each of us reaching out tentatively, knowing that the other was some sort of lifeline.

For a little while Rubin let me share a bit of his pain, and he started to let himself feel again. In the movie *The Hurricane,* which tells this story, Denzel Washington, who plays Rubin, says, "You guys are making me get loose," meaning that he was starting to hope again, that he was longing to be out, be free.

Then one day, Rubin shut down all communication. He wanted freedom itself just a little too much. Rubin would tell you himself, he got scared. His mind, not his heart, told him, "Don't dream the seemingly impossible because you know you will only be cut off at the path."

Have you ever heard yourself say something like that?

When we see an obstacle in our path and something's telling us it can't be overcome, it's usually our head talking, not our heart. Rubin had come upon an obstacle, and for some time after that, he was unable to get over it. It turned into a struggle between his head and his heart, between fear and determination, between wanting something so bad you can taste it and being so afraid of failing that you become paralyzed.

We all face these struggles. Rubin's battle with his own fear shows how each of us can become the greatest obstacle standing in the way of our own success. We can literally prevent ourselves from changing the course of our life and from doing what we truly want. Rubin was very close to not being able to respond to the miraculous coincidences that had caused our paths to cross. He almost lost the greatest fight of his life: the battle against himself. If he had given in to his fear, most likely he would still be in prison today. The coincidence of my picking up his book, being moved enough to write to him, and us actually meeting would all have been lost.

But Rubin didn't give in. Although it took him an entire year, he eventually knocked his fear to the ground by repeating to himself over and over, "Only he or she who has the courage to attempt the ridiculous can ever achieve the impossible." As Rubin explained to me later, the hardest part was that while his heart could leap over those high prison walls, his mind, which had been taken over by fear, played tricks on him. His mind controlled his thoughts and his attitude.

What happened to Rubin can sometimes happen to all of us. Fear (in his mind) was stopping him from imagining that one day he could get out of prison. He didn't have the right attitude, and he wasn't ready to believe that anything is possible if you set your mind to it.

It goes to show that in order to take advantage of coincidence and the opportunities that present themselves to you, you have to be ready at all times. You need to be able to embrace change and know it will help you achieve your goals. When you're not ready, it's all too easy to miss out on opportunities or be steered off the right course. I like to say, "You have to get yourself ready now so you won't need to waste time getting ready when opportunity knocks at the door."

Coincidence is opportunity met with preparation!

My life has been filled with an incredible number of miraculous coincidences like this one with Rubin Carter. You might be tempted to say, "Well, you were in the right place at the right time." I hear that a lot. But I have a different perspective. I was in the right time and in the right frame of mind. The place could have been just about anywhere. I think of the things that have happened in my life as miraculous because I believe that with every coincidence comes a little bit of magic. We all have miraculous coincidence in our lives. It is up to us whether or not the magic is released. The way we choose to respond to the situation will determine the outcome.

I don't know about your life, but I bet if you thought about it, you may have thought some events were purely coincidental. When they happened, did you feel the magic? Were you ready or did you miss the window of opportunity?

Coincidence often creates a domino effect!

Consider my life. My benefactors offered me the opportunity to get out of the ghetto and get an education. That was amazing. I picked up Rubin's book *The 16th Round,* which set in motion a series of events that continue to have positive consequences. If you've seen the movie *Pay It Forward,* you'll know what I'm talking about. If you haven't, the concept is simple. When someone does something good for you, rather than trying to pay that person back for his or her kindness, you pay it forward by helping someone else. As a result of all the incredible things that have happened to me, a documentary film was made about my life, and I became a public speaker to share my story with as many people as possible. As a result, I receive a great number of letters from people who have been inspired enough to write and share how my presentation helped them.

The following letter from Andrea Williams in Orleans, Ontario, is just one example.

My name is Andrea Williams and I am a vice principal with the Ottawa-Carleton District School Board. I had the pleasure and privilege of hearing you speak at our Leadership Conference in April. Words cannot accurately describe how impressed I was upon hearing your life journey, the struggles that you encountered and the perseverance that you have demonstrated—truly remarkable! As an educator, I strongly believe that it is my role not solely to teach curriculum but also to develop character in my students so that they can become responsible contributing members of society. I shared some of your background, the hurdles you faced and how you persevered with my grade six students. They were so intrigued and they were thirsty to learn more. As such, I ordered your documentary and we viewed it as a class. During the presentation you could have heard a pin drop in the classroom. We had been talking about social justice and, following the viewing of your documentary, we had a phenomenal discussion surrounding the themes that were at the forefront of the movie (i.e., perseverance, believing in oneself, the importance of family and education) ...

Your story formed the framework for our last discussions on building character. They were so enthralled with your journey that they all wanted to write you and let you know how your story has impacted their world and personal view. We would all be thrilled if you took the time to read some of our letters and to respond to us. Please know that this would mean the world to these students who see you as an instrumental figure in shaping how they see the world around them and their potential ability to achieve personal goals.

On a last note, I would personally like to thank you for reminding us that we can all achieve the "seemingly impossible" when we are open to opportunities and when we let our minds travel the road that our hearts have paved.

The letters from the students in Ms. Williams's class inspired me when I read them. Here are a few of their comments:

Your story taught me much about hope, taking risks, the importance of education and to believe in doing anything I want to do. Troy

You have no idea how much you made me realize that I am very fortunate to have the education that I do and to live in the community that I currently live in ... Whenever I feel like I can't do something, I will think of you and how you helped Hurricane Carter. Zoe

I like how you never stopped trying your best. I never have been able to do my best but ever since I saw your story I've been trying harder. Nathaniel

To take all opportunities and chances given, to believe in yourself and the power of one, to strive and do your best in school to become well educated and to persevere and never give up. These once seemed to me like phrases to keep in mind, but I never really understood them. I am ashamed to say it, but I never really cared. Now I know what an impact they can have on life and the difference they can make. For example, if you did not grasp the opportunity of education, you wouldn't be where you are today and I wouldn't be writing this letter. Nicole

All the letters I received were terrifically moving. These students' letters demonstrate to me that you never know what positive effect a coincidence that you act on today may have on others in the future.

We all share this planet together. I believe we all can have an impact on the planet, one person at a time. Every day, through my website, I receive messages and letters from people around the world. Though it takes time to get to all of them, I endeavor to personally respond to a handful of emails every day. I want to share some of them with you to underscore just how widespread the effect of coincidence can be. I have elected to reproduce the letters as I received them, unedited for grammar and spelling.

Dear Mr. Martin,

My name is Anna Veneroso and I'm an English teacher in a middle school in Northern Italy, province of Como. I've just watched the film "Hurricane" together with my students and it's very difficult to express all the feelings about your story and that of "Rubin". We were all very much impressed and breathed a sensation of freedom and justice.

As a teacher of young kids (11-14) I have always to deal with children who care more of their cellulars, computers, videogames than studying, ignoring that BOOKS may give them real POWER. This film made them reflect and think, but for how long??? I would like that this experience for them wouldn't end and that what they saw was not just a film. For this reason I would love to have a response from you (from Rubin too?): a letter, a message, even a short note to show them that really LOVE can open the doors of a prison and that WRITING can be the best way to succed in life.

I would also like to express you all my compliments and thank you for what you have done and doing for each of us!

With respect, sincerely yours,

Anna Veneroso
Via alle Carceri-Italy

Dear Mr. Martin,

I do not know if this will find its way to you, but I wanted to say a few things in hope that it will.

I just watched the movie, and followed up by reading your story. Im ashamed that it took me this long to learn. Forget the fact that a young man took on the world in freeing a wrongfully convicted man. But your story of rising from the challenges of a troubled home, a rough neighborhood, and illiteracy to become educated and successful is amazing. I feel like parts of your early life were similar to mine, and perhaps that's why your story touched me the way it did.

So I wanted to say, congratulations, and thank you. For being a great person, for your efforts with Mr. Carter, and for having the courage to rise above the things so many use as excuses to keep them down.

And thank you for the inspiration.

God Bless,

Alex Lowry

Hi Lesra,

Got your website, am so proud of you- I named my 7 month old son Lesra after watching the Hurricane- what you did was great- I was watching the movie in tears till you came in- I'ld love to hear from you (if you have sometime).
Cheers
Regards
Jane

Dear Lesra,
i am so glad to hearing from you !!!
As I read your e-mail you can not imaging how happy I was. The first thing I thought I have to tell that to somebody. And I did. I told it to some of my friends and also to my dad and my little brother, they were happy for me too and they want me to give you their best regards.

To be honest at first I did not thought that I would get a reply back. But so much better the surprise was. I want you to know what this means for me, for a young man, who get into contact with one of his biggest role model. It is like a dream come true and you make the dream come true.

Thank you Mr. Martin for being what you are. A good soul. I also want to say thank you for your words, which I really appreciate. Your words gave me something special to thought about.
! "You simply never know what can happen when you try" !
I tried something and I was successful.

So you don't have to dream your life you have to live your life; you have to live your dreams, so make your dreams come true.
I always had dreams and I always will. And I am sure that words can help to make them true.

You know words are just words but words, which you think about that are thoughts.
And thoughts are for ever and thoughts can not be stolen by anybody.

I hope you know what I am talking about.

Thanks a lot Lesra
ALEX

Dear Lesra,
My name is Madhur, I am from India. I am a musician and a High School student. As a musician I listen to allot of Music, Mainly Bob Dylan, because of whom I got to know about Rubin Hurricane Carter. I watched the movie recently too and I have been extremely touched by firstly the life of Rubin Carter and Secondly by how you both found each other through destiny. I wanted to talk to Rubin and you! Why? Is a answer I do not have, If you read this, like Rubin read your mail, please write back.
Much Love and Regards, Madhur

81

I watch the film called "The Hurricane" which is based on Rubin carter and how you helped him prove his innocence. After watching the film I read your article on "The Devastating Impact of Illiteracy." This made me think about how much I take reading and writing for granted as I learnt to read and write from a very young age. I'm currently 16 living in Wales knowing how hard you have worked from when you was in Grade 10 class telling the rest of the class your plans to become a lawyer then actually overcoming reading and writing to become and fulfilled your dream give's me the confidence and motivation to work hard enough to achieve my goals and drive to overcome the hurdles which come with it.

Thank you, Ben Jones

Hello Lesra,
I wanted to say thank you. I aspire and work towards positively impacting the world as you have.
Truly Inspired and thankful for your contribution
Jeff Armstrong

I am sure you are much too busy to respond to all of the e-mails you receive. I watched the Hurricane for the first time this weekend. I was truly inspired by what you did. I haven't done anything as big as you have (I guess its all a matter of how you look at it). I worked for a while with Literacy Kansas City teaching adults to read. I also helped a 3rd grade child get a much needed FREE prosthetic leg with free fittings until the age of 18. I try to do things to help people and I was just amazed at what you were able to do. I would LOVE to hear back from you and maybe send you a letter. If you remember how you felt with Mr. Carter first returned your letter - that is how I would feel being able to hear from you. You are truly an inspiration and after watching the Hurricane, I feel very inspired to continue to help others, as I've tried to in the past. Thank you for what you did for Mr. Carter and thank you for inspiring so many others.
    - Lisa Meland

Good Morning Lesra,

Thank you for taking the time to write me back so quickly. Again, your words are what I needed to hear. The words from your Grand Mother, "You never know unless you try." Make a lot of sense to me at this time in my life. I am scared to change my career. I am worried about finances and about how it will affect my future, in having children etc....I want to open my own business. It is a scary and exciting time all at once. I grew up in a family business and didn't really have a childhood, didn't have time with my parents because they were always busy. I do not want history to repeat itself.

Your Grand Mother is absolutely right though! I have to try... because if I don't, I will always wonder what would have happened if I did try.

I pray that I able to make the right decisions and make better choices than my parents did. Which reminds me of the sacrifice your parents made for you. I truly believe that our parents always have our best interests at heart, even if their choices caused us pain, it was all meant to be, otherwise, we wouldn't be the people we are today. I commend your parents for putting your needs first and not their sadness of losing you. That must have been gut wrenching for them. It shows how much heart they have.

I think I have to be easier on myself and realize that if I make a mistake with my children, it's okay. Life has a funny way of working things out for our highest good.

It was nice sharing with you and thanks for listening to my rambling on!!!!
Take care and many blessings to you,

~Monica~

83

Dear Lesra,

I am a white man, 32, living in Texas. I only start my letter to you in this manner to demonstrate to you how much your story and Hurricane's story moves me. I just recently have watched the movie that relayed your story, and I can honestly say you move me. Thank you for being the type of person that would pursue this type of case. Thank you for being an inspiration to not only people of color, but to people of meek beginnings. You are the type of person that truly conveys the old adage of "Only in America", except that you were fortunate enough to make the Canadian dream. I do appreciate the fact that you fought so hard and honestly to do what you thought was right. You are a credit to the Human Race. I am proud to be one of your peers. I only hope that my legacy will equal, even a little, yours. I know by now that you know I am not the only one you touched. You should know, you make me wanna do great and honorable things. Please continue to do what is right, and know that you will always be in my thoughts. If at some point in our lives, we get the chance to meet...I will undoubtedly shake your hand as a brother.

Sincerely,
Jason

PS.
Please do excuse any misspellings or grammar mistakes, as I am a software engineer.

Hi Lesra!
When I start reading about you--just an hour ago-- I thought: Oh, just another guy, I've heard all about them before!
But I was wrong. You are not just another guy. You have inspired me. Now I believe that my dreams really can come true. I believe that the reason your dreams came true, was because you believed. You had the faith, even when it was dark. Now you give the faith

to other people who need it. You are a great person. Thank you, for believing in your dreams.

Ine-Berit

P.s: I'm not that good at english, because I'm from Norway.

Each of these inspirational messages reinforces my belief that responding to a mere coincidence can have a ripple effect. That ripple can extend to the planet, enabling us to have an impact worldwide.

> *Prepare yourself to take advantage of coincidence!*

Forget about the perfect circumstances, the perfect opportunity, or the perfect situation. There's no such thing. As I've said elsewhere, you've got to start where you are, use what you've got, and do what you've got to do. More important than creating the perfect situation is being ready to make the most of whatever comes your way. Who would have thought that Rubin's decision to answer a letter from a teenage boy would eventually lead to his release from prison? As Rubin himself likes to say, "Sometimes small doors open up into very large rooms."

You have to be ready to respond to the things that happen and use the magic in every coincidence to make that happening your own. You have to be prepared to respond to people and circumstances and instances as they come your way, or the opportunity that lies within them will be lost forever. You miss out when you're not ready. In order to take advantage of coincidence and the opportunities that present themselves to you, you have to accept that they will involve change—something that is frightening to most of us. To be ready, you must be willing to accept and embrace the changes that will come. When you're not ready, it's all too easy to miss out on opportunities or to drop the ball when life throws a coincidence your way.

Promise to Take Advantage of Coincidence

*Life is about experiences. The more experiences you allow
yourself to have, the richer your life will be.*

Whether you believe it or not, coincidences happen all the time.
That's because coincidences are simply unpredicted circumstances
that we are able to take advantage of. We are simply in the right
place at the right time, ready and willing to run with the ball.

Don't believe it? According to statisticians (people who like
to calculate the odds of particular things happening), an event
that happens to only one in a billion people in a day will happen
2,000 times a year. The question is whether you will be ready for
coincidence when it comes your way.

A coincidence could change your life!

I have said time and time again that had I not met (and been
prepared to respond to) the do-gooders who took me to Toronto
and set off a chain reaction of wonderful coincidences in my life,
there would have been literally only three options for my future:
to be killed on the street (like my brother Elston was at the age
of thirty), to be an alcoholic or strung out on drugs (like so many
of the young men and women I grew up with), or locked away in
prison like my oldest brother Fru who later died from AIDS. That
is not an exaggeration. What were my chances?

Imagine if I had been too afraid to say yes. Imagine if my
parents hadn't been brave enough to let me go. Given the odds, it's
likely that I wouldn't even be alive today, never mind a university
graduate and a lawyer. Although I haven't mentioned it before, I
was not the only ghetto kid my benefactors offered this opportunity
to. They also invited another boy from the ghetto who was working
with me that summer. While I said yes to the opportunity offered,
he said no. We never kept in touch or saw each other again, but I
sometimes wonder how things turned out for him and whether he
ever questioned that decision later in his life. That's the thing about

coincidences, they provide a time-limited opportunity. If we aren't ready to act, we miss out.

Be ready to take advantage of coincidence!

We never know what can happen when we respond to the unexpected events in our lives. When we're caught off-guard by the opportunity, over-think our response, or get caught up with worrying about all of the possible complications, the moment passes us by and nothing changes. However, when we are ready to imagine the possibilities and respond in a positive way, wonderful things can happen.

The difference between those of us who take advantage of coincidence and those who don't is preparation. If we are ready when coincidence presents itself, then we will be able to embrace the situation. If we still have to get ourselves ready, we will miss out.

How do we get ready to take advantage of coincidences in our life? To start with, we need to invest time in ourselves and work on the lessons that have been presented to us (all of those important life lessons we've talked about). We also need to determine what we want from life (our goals and dreams), what our priorities are (work, family, friends, for example), what we stand for (our moral parameters), and what makes us happy (such as traveling the world, running our own business, becoming an expert in a particular field, helping others). When we've taken the time to prepare ourselves, we have a much better idea of the kinds of situations that will benefit us.

Make it easy for coincidence to find you!

Once we're ready to take advantage of coincidence, we need to make it easier for coincidence to find us. The old adage about keeping your head down with your nose to the grindstone doesn't work—at best it leads to the painful amputation of your nose. We need to make ourselves visible to others and take an interest in what is happening around us (keep your head up, make eye contact with the people you meet, and don't be afraid to strike up a conversation). The more we get involved, the more likely that we will meet people who can help us reach our goals. Likewise, when we help others, they get a better understanding of who we are (and what our goals are) and are more likely to think of us (or refer people to us) when an opportunity arises.

Jump at the chance!

Now that we're ready and looking out for coincidences in our life, there's only one more thing to do: Take action when coincidences happen. Because life can get in the way of our good intentions, it is important to train ourselves to act on opportunity. My wife, Cheryl, and I follow this philosophy in our law practice. For example, if we suddenly bump into someone whom we haven't seen in a long time or have a chance encounter that offers an interesting opportunity, we make the time then and there to see where it takes us. It could be as simple as inviting that old acquaintance to have lunch, sending an email to someone we met at a seminar to follow up on an interesting conversation, or grabbing a coffee with a person who wants to pick our brain about a new venture they are working on.

Make your own coincidence!

Of course, not everyone is satisfied with waiting for coincidence to happen. Some people go out of their way to create their own coincidences, and we can learn from their example. How do they do it? Through a number of ways. One tactic is to regularly go through their Rolodex or stacks of old business cards and touch base with people they have lost contact with to check in and see what they are up to (most people appreciate it when we take an interest in them). Another is to put themselves in new situations where they are out of their depth to some extent (pushing themselves to learn something new or overcome a fear such as public speaking or skydiving). You never know who you'll meet or what you'll learn about yourself in such instances. A third way is to constantly explore new ideas by reading books, actively participating in organizations of interest, seeking out mentors and experts to learn from, or offering to collaborate with others.

Keep yourself open to chance!

Even if you aren't ready to go out and make your own coincidences, being open to the possibilities is an important part of inviting coincidences into your life. For me, a coincidence ten years ago led to a friendship that has impacted virtually every aspect of my life. It started with a telephone call inviting me to a fundraising dinner in Vancouver, which was being organized by a fellow named Gerry Lev. I had never met Gerry, but his organization had hired Rubin Carter to be the keynote speaker for their gala evening. He knew the story behind Rubin's release from prison, so he thought it would add a whole new level of excitement to the evening if he could introduce me as a surprise guest at the conclusion of Rubin's speech. At the time, Rubin and I had been out of contact for a few years. I thought it would be a nice opportunity for a reunion so I agreed.

The evening was a smashing success. I'm positive there was not a dry eye in the house by the end of it. Even more significant for me, Gerry and his wife, Joyce Depray, turned out to be amazing people with whom I have formed an incredible bond in the years since. As a successful entrepreneur and mentor, Gerry has provided invaluable advice and guidance on my career. Most importantly, he has been a positive force and a source of inspiration as I have faced some of the most important decisions in my life.

"Lesra, you have to be able to imagine the outcome you want here," he told me when I confided to him that Cheryl and I were trying for a baby with only a 20 percent chance that I could father a child. Today, we have not one but two beautiful daughters. Gerry and Joyce spoil them. Needless to say, I am grateful for the coincidence that brought Gerry into my life.

Pay attention to the chance encounters and unexpected situations that happen every day and ask yourself, "Why did I bump into this particular person today?" "Is there something in this situation that I could use in my life right now?" Your brain is hard wired to find patterns and connections, so promise yourself to take advantage of coincidence. Soon, you'll start to see opportunities where you never noticed them before.

Part 2
Dreams, Determination, and Discipline

We all want to have a good life. We human beings have been given the amazing ability to dream. We can see possibilities that lie beyond the life we have now, and we can imagine ourselves living in that new reality. Even more amazing, we have also been given the ability to pursue and achieve those dreams, using our powers of determination and discipline.

- *Dreams.* Dreams are the imaginings of what we can make happen in our lives. By dreaming we generate hope for the future, and with hope comes possibility. Dreams can be big and seem unrealistic at first glance, but they fill us with desire and inspiration and that is their purpose. When we are too afraid to hope and dream, we deprive ourselves of the opportunity to make a better life. Allow yourself to dream.

- *Determination.* Although dreams are free, the achievement of our dreams often requires a great investment of effort on our part. And when we dream big, undoubtedly, obstacles come into our path. To keep going, we will need both dedication and determination. Determination is the grit that gets us to our goal. With determination at our back, we can push beyond the resistance in our mind that tells us "give up, let it go" and find a way to carry on toward fulfilling our dreams. Determination gives us the ability to get back up when we have fallen, to keep swinging away despite how the odds may be stacked against us. Determination gives us the strength to bring our dreams into being.

- *Discipline.* Discipline is the ability we all possess to stay focused on our dreams and to remain determined in the pursuit of our goals—even in the face of temptation. In the world we live in, it's all too easy to find shortcuts, to focus on indulging our immediate desires, to lay aside our principles and forget about our purpose. Discipline is the force that keeps us on the right path, the knife that slashes through our fears, and the voice that whispers to hold strong when we begin to bend under the weight of our goals.

I strongly believe we are only capable of dreaming things we can actually accomplish. If we can believe, we can achieve. Unfortunately, sometimes the achievement of our dreams is hampered by our circumstances, our surroundings, and even our own mindset. To succeed, we must be able to draw on the passion that fuels our dream, to tap into the determination and discipline that will help us make the right decisions along the way, and to spare no effort in our pursuit of the goals that will form the foundation of a better life.

8

Imagine the Best: The Importance of Never Knowing You Couldn't

One of the side effects of growing up is finding out what we *can't* do. We learn to follow rules. Gradually we limit our potential to things we're told we *can* do. As young children, though, we didn't put so many limitations on ourselves. Because we had the ability to imagine the best, we still believed that anything was possible, and we allowed ourselves to dream big dreams.

Just the other day my wife and our six-year-old daughter went to pick up our four-year-old from preschool. As they approached the adjacent playground, the six-year-old ran ahead to meet her little sister while mom lagged behind. When the four-year-old saw her older sister coming to get her, she came running toward her, and they both headed for the car. The younger child had yet to realize that mom was coming too. So when mom came into view from behind the vehicle, the four-year-old looked up at her older sister in surprise and said, "I thought you had come to pick me up by yourself."

Realizing herself to be much more grownup and worldly, big sister simply gave her one of those "older and wiser" looks that older siblings save for these occasions and nonchalantly said, "I can't drive silly."

"Oh," said the younger one.

Believing anything is possible!

When my wife told me this story, my immediate reaction was that it was funny how the younger child would have thought nothing of it had her six-year-old sister hopped into the driver's seat and proceeded to drive her home. For me, this story underscores how kids interact with the world around them. Their first instinct isn't to think that they can't do something. To a kid, anything is possible. They don't begin thinking they can't do something until we start telling them they can't.

My second thought, when my wife told me this story, was a feeling of fear regarding how easy it would be for my younger child to attempt to drive. She didn't think anything of the possibility that her six-year-old sister potentially could have driven on her own to pick her up.

Kids don't have fear in the same way we adults do. It goes to show that thinking you can't do something—and even fear itself—is a learned behavior. Wouldn't it be great if we, as adults, could retain that childlike ability to think that anything is possible? Wouldn't it be great to retain a little bit of the freedom of ignorance and innocence of not knowing that you can't? What could we achieve if we were free of the fear of not being able to do something? What heights could we rise to if we were able to suspend disbelief?

As adults, we stay in our comfort zone. Kids explore. We don't! We need to challenge ourselves to do things outside the box and outside our comfort zone. Great things don't happen to those who are cautious and guarded. They happen to people who are willing to explore and risk.

I was thinking about how difficult it sometimes is to push myself outside my comfort zone. At what age, I wondered, do we lose the attitude of thinking that anything is possible? When do we go from a state of thinking *I can* to *I can't*? Although our four-year-old daughter didn't realize that her older sister couldn't drive, our six-year-old daughter already knew she couldn't. It really made me stop and think about all the limiting beliefs we pass on to our children. It also made me realize we need to unlearn some things because we have become jaded, afraid, and restricted in our thinking. We keep these fears in our mind and allow them to limit the way we experience the world and what we are willing to try. Rather than taking a chance and trying something new, we end up telling ourselves: "I can't do that!" "I don't know how." "I'd be crazy to try."

Stop imagining the worst!

Isn't it strange in life how we often imagine the worst? Do you ever catch yourself doing that? I know that I do. The other day I had a bad case of indigestion. As I felt the discomfort start to radiate outward, the first thing that entered my mind (I even said it to my wife) was, "You know, they say that a heart attack starts with the same sensation as indigestion." Looking back at that moment, I realize just how easy it is for our thinking to take us down the wrong road, carried away with fantasies about the worst that could happen. When you take that road, before you know it, you'll be planning the guest list for your funeral.

That's the kind of thinking we need to check at the door.

It's time to imagine the best!

Recently, I shared a personal story with an audience. I told them that one of the most difficult battles in my life was learning to read and write. When I was finished, a fellow put up his hand and asked, "How did you do it? How did you manage to overcome such difficulties in a situation where everything was against you?"

Without having to think too much about it, I responded, "Everything started to change when I began to imagine the best." It's true. By deciding to imagine the best, I immediately stopped focusing on the problems in my life and started to look for positive things that I could begin to build on. When I started to imagine the best, doors began to open, and I saw new possibilities.

When you imagine the best, the best begins to happen. In the same way, when you imagine the worst, that's what you get because it's all you can see through your negative-colored glasses. When you focus on the negative, even with the good things, you find yourself looking closely to find the downside or problem. Despite the fact that things seem to be going your way, you undoubtedly find yourself saying, "This can't last!" "I know something is going to go wrong, it always does." "It's too good to be true."

Have you been there? I know I have. I have heard those words— too many times. I used to hear them so much I couldn't move.

> *Sometimes we need an attitude adjustment!*

I failed at my first job as a waiter. I didn't have the right attitude about what I was doing, and my coworkers and the customers picked up on that. I took what I learned from my failure and turned it into a good start in my second job in retail. Two and a half months after being hired as a salesman in a men's clothing shop, I was managing my own store.

What made the difference? As a salesperson on commission, I soon realized that responding to the needs of customers wasn't necessarily about selling. More important than that, it was about listening, understanding, and wanting to serve and fulfill their needs. To help me be my best, I developed a philosophy that I called, "Look good, feel good, sell good." The philosophy is based on the idea that, in order to respond to the needs of my customers, I needed to be in the right frame of mind.

To get into that frame of mind, I had to make sure I took the time each day to fulfill my own needs—whether it was getting up early enough to have a relaxing shower before work, taking the time to have a good breakfast, or treating myself to a new tie or a pair of shoes to make me feel sharp—so that I would be ready to focus on the needs of my customers.

The philosophy paid off. Although I was only working part-time because of my university studies, the boss offered me the job of manager. When I asked her why she had chosen me over several other salespeople who had been with the company for a year or more, she pointed out that during the time I had been working there, I was the only staff member with a consistent record of sales.

Accepting the promotion, I used my "look good, feel good, sell good" philosophy to motivate and train the rest of the staff. We became an unstoppable team. As a result, when I was again presented with the opportunity to move up to a higher level of management within the company, my acceptance was contingent on whether they would permit me to take my whole team with me. They agreed.

Although I eventually left the retail business to finish my education, I continue to be guided by the "look good, feel good, sell good" philosophy even today. It has been an important part of my success in both my law practice and as a public speaker.

> *Change your attitude, change your life!*

You've heard this expression: "Attitude is everything." Our attitude affects the way we experience everything in life. When I replaced my negative thoughts with something positive, it changed the way I looked and how I lived my life. When I changed my attitude toward the world, good things began to happen. I discovered possibilities I hadn't been able to see before.

When you are healthy in your mind and healthy in your thoughts, that is what you're going to attract. You remember how we talked about the domino effect in the last chapter? That effect also applies to attitude. As I grew older and realized what a blessing my benefactors had been in my life, I asked them what made them want to help me in the first place. Without hesitation, they told me it was because of my attitude. They had met me at the Greenpoint Environmental Testing Lab, where I had a job the summer I was fifteen. They were taken by my interest in them as Canadians, my quick comebacks when they joked with me, and my self-assurance when I boldly announced to them, "I'm going to be an attorney someday."

A lot of my confidence and positive attitude at that point in my life was the result of Grandma Costa's influence on me. She showed me that I could believe in myself and do anything with my life, if I set my mind to it. I'm thankful that Grandma Costa was able to imagine the best for me. She knew there would be significant obstacles in my way, but she never once discouraged me from believing that I could go to college and become an attorney.

I'm grateful too that my benefactors imagined the best for me, even when they learned I had the reading and writing level of a second-grade student. Through all the months I struggled, thinking I was incapable of learning and wracked with self-doubt, they believed I was capable of great things—and, eventually, I believed too.

Promise to Imagine the Best

To accomplish great things, we must not only act, but also dream; not only plan, but also believe. Anatole France

Each one of us sees things as we want to see them. We make them what we want them to be. That's fine when we take an optimistic outlook, but we are equally capable of imagining and expecting the very worst to happen. If your view of the world and your place in it doesn't inspire you and make you feel optimistic about the future, it's time to look for a new perspective. Allowing yourself to imagine the best not only lets you change the way you look at life—by getting you to visualize more positive, hopeful outcomes—it also begins to change the way you respond to the people and situations you encounter. Positive images change the way your life really is, for the better.

Have you ever watched a truly great basketball player like LeBron James when he is in the zone? Noticed the way he moved down the court, positioning himself to receive the ball, anticipating every move his opponent is going to make until he gets within range, and then BAM! He takes his shot, and you know he's going to sink that basket every time. You can bet he has practiced his moves on the court for just that moment, but he also has visualized the scenario in his mind over and over—a thousand times or more.

In the same way, have you ever woken up in the morning and felt great? You know those mornings. You wake up rested and refreshed and jump out of bed feeling so optimistic and happy that you can't help but feel something great is going to happen. You hummed while you got yourself ready for work. You were happy with the way you looked. And even though you smiled and said good morning to everyone you met along the way, you got to work early enough to organize your schedule before things got under way. It was just an all-around fantastic day. You resolved nagging problems. You were amazingly productive. You were untouchable.

Let's extend that scenario to 24/7 so you can be your best all day, every day. Sound exhausting? Think again. It is energizing.

Put yourself in the picture!

See what I mean? Imagine it, feel it, embrace it. See yourself waking up and having that kind of day every day. Think about what kind of life that would be. You're there—mind and body—that is all it takes.

Perception (what we think about things) affects everything. Because our subconscious mind doesn't differentiate between what is really happening to us and what we perceive to be happening, we can actually change our reality by changing the way we perceive things.

We live in a complex world. Every time we turn around, things are changing—new technologies and innovations, new rules and regulations, new threats and concerns. With life's fast pace, it is easy to feel insignificant. Large corporate and government bureaucracies remind us of it. The incredible force of nature reinforces it. Even the breathtaking beauty of Mother Nature can emphasize it. We can end up feeling like a mere pawn in the game of life. But put yourself in the picture and checkmate—perception affects everything. You are part of the bigger picture where every move you make can have a ripple effect. Your attitude and your perception of your role in life is the real determining factor for how big an impact you can have on the world around you.

When we can imagine great things, they can happen!

It is amazing what can happen when we are able to put ourselves in the picture. When we will ourselves to be on the path. Many times in my life I had difficulty putting myself in the picture. Although I had always dreamed of becoming a lawyer, at the age of twenty if someone had told me I would go to law school, I would have said, "Yeah, right!" At twenty-five, if someone had told me I would go on and become a prosecutor, I would have said, "Yeah, right!" And even after I became a prosecutor (with all the challenges I had already been able to overcome), if someone had told me I would go on to become a professional speaker and inspire others with my story, I definitely would have said, "Yeah, right!"

Today, I believe that anything is possible. I have learned not to allow my own thoughts or perceptions to limit the opportunities that come my way. Earlier this year, I was approached by the Canadian Broadcasting Corporation (CBC) and asked if I would be open to the possibility of doing a show on weekday mornings. Now, I never imagined there might be a radio talk show in my future, but once I listened to the proposal, I could see myself in that picture, doing it and loving it.

Other opportunities have come my way recently. I was invited to work with the Vancouver chapter of Democrats Abroad (which represents American citizens around the world who support the Democratic Party) and to consider starting a chapter of the organization in the interior of British Columbia. I am also approached on a regular basis to speak to groups about the importance of literacy and education—both topics I am passionate about. Yet none of these things would have found their way to me if I wasn't able to open myself to the possibilities, if I wasn't able to imagine the best for myself—which emphasizes the point that what we are capable of imagining for ourselves inevitably affects everything. So promise to always imagine the best.

9

The Shadows That Hang Over Us: Learning from the Past and Letting It Go

Our past is like a shadow, hovering over the present. Depending on our perspective, that shadow can be a dark cloud or a gentle reminder, our closest friend or our greatest enemy. For many years I hated my past and I endeavored to shut it out or try to wish it away. Yet, no matter how hard I tried, when I woke each morning, the first thing that played through my mind was the same old images of the life I had tried to leave behind in the ghetto of New York. It was as if my brain had an auto-rewind switch, so the moment I was conscious, I would be back in the ghetto, feeling the full force of those old emotions of fear, anger, frustration, and hopelessness closing in on me.

In university I was particularly frustrated with my burden of memories and resentful that my fellow students didn't have to deal with the same thing. While out of one eye I could see the beautiful University of Toronto campus and my life in the present moment, out of the other eye, I always saw the shadows of my past and the difficulties I had faced there.

> *You can't change the past, but you*
> *can change your perspective!*

From my perspective, the other students' lives were uncomplicated and carefree (with parents to pay their tuition and plenty of time for parties and socializing). They had never experienced the kind of turmoil I had. I was desperately jealous of them. For a time I lost sight of the fact that, despite the different paths that had brought us to campus, I had access to the same bright future I envied them for having.

But that future wasn't going to happen for me if I couldn't resolve the two competing elements of the past and the present. Eventually, as I began to realize I was banging my head against the wall by trying to wish away my past, I started to understand that in some ways I had an advantage over many of the same students I envied. Because of the hardships I had overcome, I had developed many strengths and resources they might never possess.

Eventually I came to terms with my past. I finally realized and accepted that I am made up of two very different people: the boy who lived in the ghetto in New York and the young man who seized an opportunity to change his destiny and today lives a life filled with promise and good fortune.

It has taken time to find a peaceful coexistence between the two parts of myself, but the realization has been vital to my sanity and sense of well-being. The turning point came when I was finally able to recognize that I was richer for the experiences I had lived through; they offered valuable lessons I could use to make my life better. The memory of those experiences also provides me with an important reminder to appreciate all that I have and never to take it for granted.

> *The past doesn't have to be overwhelming!*

Once you change your perspective, something curious happens. You begin to notice that you're not dwelling nearly so much on the bad things. Instead you begin to focus on some of the good memories.

As I began to look at my past from a new perspective, I was also able to come to terms with some of the anger and resentment I felt toward my parents, particularly my father, whom I blamed for moving our family to Bed-Stuy.

In letting go of my anger, I could recall some of the good times we once shared and remember the person my father had once been. Before our problems began and even before the workplace accident that injured his back and took away his livelihood, my father was a playful, positive force in our family. What I remember most about "Pops" during that time is how all of the kids were attracted to him and how much he, in turn, loved playing the part of the benevolent father. Other kids in the neighborhood often told me how lucky I was that my dad actually lived with us still, since so many of them didn't have a dad at home.

I also remember that my father gave away money when he was working, and he always had candy, a dollar bill, or loose change to hand out. In fact, one of his favorite things on a Saturday morning was to lift up the window when he woke up and chuck handfuls of change that he'd collected during the week into the yard where all of us kids we're playing. You could see the sheer joy on his face at the sight of kids tripping over each other trying to pick up as much as they could. He'd yell encouragement and point to a coin saying, "That one's for ...", or "Make sure the little ones get some too!"

During those early years of my life when he was still happy and sober, I looked forward to every moment when my father was home, enthralled by his ability to make everything fun. I especially looked forward to Friday afternoons when he would come home from work, bringing along a couple of buddies to play basketball using the hoop in our backyard. He always picked me to be on his team. During those games he'd offer a two dollar bet to any takers that I couldn't make a certain shot.

"Who wants to bet that Lesra can't do it?" he'd yell out gleefully, knowing the odds were stacked in his favor. What he knew, but many of these friends didn't, is that I'd become quite proficient at throwing a basketball backward over my head. Nine times out of ten, I'd nail the shot from just about anywhere on the court, and my dad would collect the winnings to be shared between us.

I'm thankful for these happy memories of my father. The ability to hold onto the positive aspects of my past has allowed me to build bridges between the difficult times in Bed-Stuy and the much happier life I live today with my wife and children of my own.

> *Allow the past to be a support not a burden!*

Have you ever seen the shadow of a person walking in front of you? At a certain time of day, their entire shadow is visible standing right beside them. It's as though there are two of the same person, one standing upright and the other on a rakish angle. I am comforted when I am lucky enough to catch a glimpse of my own shadow. It always makes me feel as if I am not alone. I have come to feel the same sense of comfort with my past.

You can't shake a shadow. And I have learned that you can't shake the past either. But you can choose what effect it will have on your life. I've talked before about how we are all born with the pieces of our puzzle. Putting the first major piece of my life's puzzle in place involved coming to terms with a difficult past. I came to realize that how I viewed my experiences would either stop me in my tracks or help me move on with my life. So I began to think of my past as a friend and a reminder of the way things could have been if I hadn't been lucky enough to escape the ghetto.

In the most positive ways my past began to shape my attitude and put into perspective the challenges in my present that I had been viewing as insurmountable. When I remembered what it was like to be hungry all the time and live with the constant fear of being attacked by gang members such as Eric and Julius, suddenly the concerns I had in my present life seemed a lot less daunting.

> *Even the most negative experiences*
> *can have a positive impact!*

Over the years I have had to overcome many shadows. One of the biggest was my survivor guilt. I think we have survivor guilt because we know how difficult life is for those we have left behind.

Another shadow is the image of my oldest brother beating up on my dad for taking his fists to our mother—the violence of the past can have a real hold on your psyche.

For many years after, I worried that I would repeat the mistakes my parents had made. I remember an incident with one of my first serious girlfriends, Pauline. I was lying in bed with her one morning, and as I rolled over I accidentally hit her in the forehead with my elbow. Although she was sound asleep at the time, she automatically flinched away from me (as if she was accustomed to having to protect herself from unprovoked attacks). Suddenly it took me right back to Bed-Stuy and my own mother's response to my father hitting her. Hitting Pauline with my elbow had been a simple accident, yet I felt guilty about it in ways that I couldn't even understand. It was as if my mind was playing a trick. For weeks afterward I kept wondering, *Is my dad in me? Will I end up being like him?*

> *You can't erase the past, so use it to help you grow!*

Although I eventually came to realize that I was not my father, the reality of growing up in an environment where my parents were always drinking and fighting had a significant impact on my approach to confrontation. From the time I was very young, I have gone out of my way to avoid arguments, heated discussions, and conflict of all kinds. Such avoidance, as an adult, doesn't always make it easy to communicate effectively and solve problems. This is particularly true in my marriage. My wife, Cheryl (who thankfully is very patient with me), constantly tries to reinforce the point that respectful disagreements and confrontation can be healthy and productive if they lead us to a better understanding of one another and assist us in resolving issues that push us apart. Despite her consistent reassurance and my best efforts to change my behavior, my first response to conflict is often still one of rigidity and withdrawal—a reaction that underscores the need to keep working on those issues from the past until we are able to overcome them.

> *You can find your way in spite of your circumstances!*

I can't forget when I fell five stories off that building at the age of thirteen. The memory of it reminds me every day how much I do want to live. When I realized that I was still alive in the hospital after my fall, I was disappointed. In contrast, my life now is full of dreams and promise. I appreciate every single moment.

> *Everything hinges on our ability*
> *to focus on the positive!*

I still wake up each morning with thoughts about my life in Bed-Stuy, even to this very day. The only difference now is I am no longer overcome by feelings of dread and fear. I perceive the past differently. Instead of being a weight around my neck, like an albatross, my past supports me, shores me up, and nurtures me. As I often say, there are two sides to every coin. So, today, instead of dwelling on the frustration that once filled my mind whenever I think about my years in the ghetto, I'm looking at the other side of the coin and seeing the great life I have built with the strengths I gained there.

Promise to Learn from the Past and Let It Go

If you look back too much, you will soon be headed that way!

No matter how much we believe we may want to leave the past behind us, moving on and changing our lives can be difficult. I remember when I first arrived in Toronto with the opportunity to get an education, I had been given a real chance, a shot at a great life. I knew it, but the realization produced such a gripping fear in me that I almost blew it.

At times during those first months, I was so scared I couldn't move. And then when I did move, I did all the wrong things. I got caught up in listening to the little voice in my head that kept telling me things like, *You don't belong here, who do you think you are?* and *You better just give up and go home now before these people realize what a fraud you are and send you back themselves.* For every step I was able to take in the right direction, that negative voice in my head would drag me two steps backward.

To move forward, we have to make peace with our past!

For a good part of my life I have felt there were two of me: the ghetto kid my benefactors saw great potential in who went on to become a lawyer, public speaker, and all around outgoing successful community member; and the other me, the guy I see in the mirror each morning who vividly recalls every aspect of living a much different, more difficult life—and has the scars to prove it. For some time this dichotomy proved to be more than a little unnerving for me as I struggled with conflicting ideas about which one of those people was really me and worried that I would never be able to reconcile the two parts of my life.

I have since learned that they are both me—parts of the same person and inseparable. I can't simply shrug off the person I was like an old coat, but I also don't have to live a life where I am constantly haunted by flashbacks from my years in the ghetto. The past is a piece of our puzzle. Finding out where it fits in our present life and how we can use the lessons we have learned from it is important work that we all have to do.

The past is always open to interpretation!

How we perceive the past is often more important than what happened there. As I've mentioned earlier, for a long time, I could only focus on the negative aspects of my life in Bed-Stuy, as if there were no happy times in my family, but that's not how it really was. Once I started to look for the positive and understand the tremendous difficulties my parents faced and the sacrifices they made, I began to take a different view and could recall the good times we shared. I also came to realize that it was up to me to decide whether I wanted to interpret the past in a way that helped me or hurt me.

How we interpret the past is important. Why? Precisely because when we interpret what has happened to us in the past, we decide whether we are going to be the hero or the victim in the story we are creating. If you think about it, in every story you've ever read (and every story that's been read to you), bad things inevitably happened to the hero. But what sets the hero apart from the other characters in the story (those who end up getting killed or written out of the action) is that the hero chooses to use the lessons he or she has learned from facing up to adversity to help him or her achieve an important goal. Without hardships to test the heroes, we wouldn't even be able to identify who the real heroes in the story are. It is the same in our own lives. If we believe that the events in our past were put in our path to help us grow, we will be able to extract the lessons we can use and then let go.

Don't get hung up on mistakes!

We all make wrong choices now and then, but we can't allow those mistakes to hold us back or cause us to second-guess our own judgment. Work on accepting the choices you've made. As long as you can be proud of the person you are inside—and believe me, you already know if you can or not—you have to trust in your ability to make good choices and believe in yourself. Although you will always face challenges and changes in your life along the way, understand that those challenges and changes will help you find the right path for you. As long as you focus on keeping yourself headed in the right direction and promise to learn from the past and let it go, nothing will ever hold you back.

10

Life's a Challenge: Remember Your Promise and Stay Focused

Many events can cause us to get off track in our lives: disappointment, illness, injury, even success if it causes us to become self-important and lose our way.

When I fell from the roof at age thirteen, I had no real will or determination to live. In contrast, after my second fall while camping, all I could think about was how much I wanted to live. The difference between those two times in my life is that, when I was thirteen, I didn't have anything to hope for or work toward. I didn't have anything to keep me focused.

Yet in my early thirties, I had achieved my dream of becoming a lawyer. I was practicing law as a Crown Prosecutor, which was very exciting to me. Additionally, I was newly married and felt I was embarking on a whole new stage of my life. Everywhere I looked, I saw opportunity. The potential that I saw in myself gave me the determination to fight when my body wanted to give up after I tripped on that tent peg and was hospitalized.

> *When we get knocked down, we have to get back up and keep going!*

We all need to fight battles every now and then. We all lose sight of our dreams every now and then. We all imagine the worst instead of the best every now and then. We all face challenges, hurdles, obstacles, and difficulties in life. If we let them, these barriers can limit us and stop us from achieving our dreams. When I awoke in the hospital after the surgery that saved me from becoming a quadriplegic, there was no thought in my mind of giving up. I was going to do whatever it took to be able to walk out of that hospital room and get on with my life. I had fought too hard to overcome the obstacles in my life to let one more stop me.

As long as we are willing to get up and keep fighting, nothing can stop us. Failure is an inevitable part of life, part of the learning process. If you don't believe me, I challenge you to name one champion who has made it to the top of their sport without ever losing a competition, one tycoon who has never had a business failure, one hero who has never had a moment of weakness. We are all human, we all fall down, and we all fail at some point. What we choose to learn from those failures and what we ultimately choose to do after we fall down is what determines whether or not we make it to the destination we have set for ourselves.

> *When we lose perspective, we need to remind ourselves of our purpose!*

No matter what kind of work we do, we should all remember that we have a role to play in how society functions and in making a contribution in the world. With how busy we all are in our everyday lives and all we have to do, it is easy for us to lose sight of how significant our contribution is, to forget our real reason for doing what we do, and simply end up feeling like a cog in the wheel, putting in time and being carried along by the current.

So what's wrong with going with the flow? The problem is that what we do every day affects the lives of others. People depend on us to do a good job (no matter what that job may be). If we're not feeling sharp, on our game, and motivated to do our best, we can get sloppy, make hasty decisions, overlook important details, or make mistakes that harm others. Imagine the impact if a patient gets the wrong prescription, if poor communication causes a workplace accident, or if an accounting error causes a small company to lose its biggest client and go under as a result. Everything we do matters to someone.

As a lawyer who handles a good number of personal injury cases, my purpose is to advocate for my clients and provide them with the best legal representation I can to ensure that they get a fair hearing and an equitable settlement. If I'm just putting in my time "doing my job" or if I'm distracted by other concerns when I need to be focused on my clients, there's a good chance that I'm going to miss something crucial. My client will suffer as a result.

Every cog in the wheel is important. When a cog is broken or missing, the wheel can no longer turn smoothly and fulfill its purpose. If you feel yourself drifting or uninspired in your job, it's probably time to check your perspective. Take some time to remind yourself of all the reasons you chose your career and what it is you want to accomplish—for yourself and for everyone whose life you touch with your work.

> *Don't be too invested in a certain way of thinking!*

Being flexible in the face of change is difficult for many people, even during the best of times. One of the best books I have read on dealing with change is by Dr. Spencer Johnson, called *Who Moved My Cheese?* If you haven't read it, I suggest you spend an hour and a half doing so. It's a quick read and a great book. The author uses cheese as a metaphor for all the things we want in life—whether it is a good job, a loving relationship, money, nice possessions, health, or simply spiritual peace of mind. The four characters in the book are looking for cheese in the "maze," which represents the paths we can go down to find the things we want in our life.

As the story begins, the characters are living a happy life filled with an abundance of cheese. With everything they could ever want within reach, they have no worries and feel no need to explore beyond the confines of their comfort zone. But then suddenly, without notice, their whole world changes when they wake up one day to discover that all of the cheese has disappeared. With no cheese and no understanding of where the cheese has gone, they don't know what to do. They begin to starve and become very unhappy.

Eventually, one of characters decides to take action. As a result, he learns to deal with the changed circumstances. By imagining that another world of abundance and happiness must lie somewhere "out there," he finds the will to make his way through the maze. Along the way, he discovers cheese in different places, so he writes on the maze walls, telling any others who might travel that way what he has learned from his experience. He hopes that one day his friend, who was too afraid to join him in his journey, will find the courage to follow behind in his footsteps.

Unfortunately, the friend is too paralyzed by fear to get himself moving. He is too upset by the changes in his life. He can't imagine the best. He can't accept that change is inevitable. Instead, he becomes angry and resentful, so he never moves.

> *In the face of adversity, flex your flexibility muscle!*

Change in life is difficult for many people to deal with—and when that change appears to set us on a course filled with hurdles and obstacles, it becomes all the more difficult to come to terms with. In the wake of challenging times, the first thing we often seem to lose is our ability to be flexible. We begin to fear change itself. Before we know it, we lose sight of our dreams and begin to imagine the worst instead of the best.

I have often wondered what makes some individuals who face the most horrific circumstances in life rise above those circumstances, meet challenges, and deal with change and adversity head on. How can they continue to think positive thoughts and strive toward something that appears unattainable? All of my research and experience points to the fact that these people have a deep belief in the power of one individual to make a great difference in the world. Here I am thinking about heroic people such as Hurricane Carter and Nelson Mandela, who endured imprisonment; Terry Fox, Christopher Reeve, and Rick Hansen, who all suffered debilitating physical injury and yet rose above it to give something wonderful to the world.

Maybe it's true. Maybe we all need a certain amount of pain or dissatisfaction to motivate us to deal with change and adversity. I recognize in each one of these people a passionate commitment, an incredible courage, and conviction. If we are to learn one thing from these souls of inspiration, it is this: In order to deal with adversity and challenges head on, you have to be flexible and you have to be able to believe that nothing can stop you, that nothing is impossible. When you hold your goal in your mind and push everything else aside, there is nothing to distract you or stand in your way. That's where the magic is.

Look at what happened in my life when I started to focus on the positive and really work at learning to read and write. Look at what happened to Rubin when he allowed himself to believe that he could be free again. As I've said before, being flexible and focused means we have to start where we are, work with what we've got, and do what we've got to do.

> ## We all face challenges!

Sometimes in life, we can begin to feel that we are just a cog in the wheel. We lose perspective on how our role helps the larger wheel to move. When that happens, we can end up putting in time, thinking that we don't make a difference, or begin acting in ways that are inconsistent with our values (for example, not following through on commitments, doing things that are counterproductive as a way of showing our dissatisfaction, or undermining the progress of others).

> ## Stop, reflect, re-evaluate!

How can we avoid getting disillusioned? Sometimes we have to remind ourselves that the world works best when we work together and have faith in our role in making the wheel turn. Look for ways to renew and reenergize your commitment by reaching out to others. Offer input on how things could work better or organize an event where problems (and potential improvements) could be discussed. Being proactive is much more healthy and empowering than complaining or focusing on the negative. When we work on overcoming our feelings of being disconnected and dissatisfied, it is easier to get back to a place where we can be effective and productive.

> *We can lose sight of our intentions!*

The busier we are, the harder it is to stay focused on what is important. When we get caught up in all of the things we need to do, it's not unusual to begin to lose sight of what we are trying to accomplish—our original purpose. Even when we are focused on keeping the promises we have made to ourselves, a lot of unexpected things can happen along the way. How we choose to deal with the challenges that present themselves is the key. If we don't stay focused, we can lose sight of our intentions and get knocked off course.

> *Don't forget to "stay loose"!*

When it comes to summing up how we can remain focused on goals and still be flexible enough to handle the challenges that arise, I've always liked the expression, "You've got to stay loose." Just like a boxer who is facing an opponent in the ring, we don't always know what life will throw at us, so we have to keep our goals in mind while also being flexible enough to dodge the punches that we know are going to come our way as we fight to fulfill the promises we've made.

Promise to Stay Focused on Your Goals

The big secret in life is that there is no big secret. Whatever your goal, you can get there if you're willing to work.
Oprah Winfrey

One of the sayings my grandmother always used when I was young is, "Life will throw you curveballs, but if you continue to swing away, you just never know when you might hit a home run." All through her life, Granny has practiced what she preached, and because of that she has been an inspiration in my life. Even with the hardships she has endured, I don't recall even one time when she let circumstances get the better of her. She always stayed focused on what needed to be done, on taking care of business, and on taking care of the family. That's the kind of determination I try to emulate in my life.

Many things will try to come between you and that home run!

As I'm sure you know all too well, it's not always easy for us to keep swinging, to stay focused on our goals. In addition to all the little distractions that come our way every day and the bigger, sometimes life-changing events that get in the way of our plans, we also have to navigate around the people (however well-meaning they may be) who would deter or dissuade us from reaching our goals.

Many times in my life people have tried to persuade me to lower my expectations and to work toward something more realistic. I have also, on occasion, been told to give up on certain dreams or goals altogether because they just can't happen.

I say, "Don't tell me that I can't because I don't believe you."

The way I see it, I've beaten the odds so many times and accomplished or come through so many things that others believed to be impossible, I can't *not* keep swinging away at my dreams. We never know what we are capable of until we have tested every one of our limits. Never give up just because someone else doesn't believe you can do it.

With determination, anything is possible!

To me, the great gift about the movie *The Hurricane* (a good part of which focuses on how my benefactors and I helped to free Rubin Carter from prison) is that it demonstrates what is possible when we focus on doing the right thing. It is a story about the power in each of us to achieve the seemingly impossible; it is a story about turning failure into success and adversity into triumph. Above all else, it is a story about determination.

Years ago, long before all the movie stuff, back to the day when Rubin's conviction was finally overturned after the many years we spent working on his case, I came up to embrace Rubin, excited and in disbelief at the same time, saying: "We did it! We did it! Can you believe it? We did it!"

"But there is one thing I need to know," I told him as I began to calm down, "How come you believed in us? Why did you eventually allow us, complete strangers, into your life?"

"Lez," he told me. "I have always believed that small doors can sometimes open into very large rooms, but in order to take advantage of the opportunity that lies beyond each one of those doors, we have to have the right attitude; we need to believe ... I had to learn that."

Let others inspire you!

I am always inspired by the example set by immigrants who come here from all around the world. Their determination to make a better life, even in the face of tremendous challenges, is something we could all learn from. My friend Bal Brar is a perfect example. Like so many others who arrived here with only their dreams of a better life, Bal started out with absolutely nothing when she came to Canada for an arranged marriage.

Discovering that her new husband didn't share the same drive, dedication and vision of achievement, Bal took it upon herself to earn a living by accepting whatever work she could get. Over the next decade, she worked her fingers to the bone and saved all that she could as she cared for her young family of three children. Seeing a business of her own as her only way to get ahead and provide a stable home for her children, Bal took the money she had scraped together and bought a Subway franchise. Because of her hard work, the store did very well, and eventually Bal was able to sell it for a good profit.

Now you might think that the story would end there with Bal and her family living happily ever after. But it doesn't. One day, while traveling through Pender Harbour on British Columbia's Sunshine Coast, Bal spotted a rundown, dilapidated old hotel and pub that had been closed for years. Seeing the potential of the location and not being one to shy away from a challenge, Bal bought the property and renovated it from top to bottom over a period of a few years. Today, it is a wonderful little resort with a great restaurant that has become a go-to spot for locals and tourists alike. Everyone who has seen the transformation marvels at Bal's vision and what she has been able to achieve through her own determination.

What I find remarkable about Bal and so many other immigrants is that they are able to come here with little more than a tremendous work ethic and accomplish amazing things (despite obvious disadvantages) at the same time many natural-born citizens of both Canada and the United States complain about a lack of opportunity. The lesson we can learn from people like Bal is that there is always opportunity if we are willing to look for it (it may not be in the most obvious places). There is always opportunity if we are willing to do the work required (that's the part that trips up so many of us). There is always opportunity if we are determined to remain focused on our goals (we need to keep swinging).

We have to use the potential we were born with!

My story is not unique. There is nothing unique about my ability, nothing unique about my brain, and nothing particularly unique about the opportunities I have had—it all comes down to what we do with what we've got. How do we use the potential we're born with? How do we respond when opportunity comes our way? I decided that the best course of action for me was to take the opportunity and run with it.

We all have the potential to achieve our dreams. The important thing to remember is that no matter how difficult the challenge, no matter how daunting the task appears to be, no matter how great the odds, we can't give up. The going may be rough. It may even get us down, but we can hit that home run if we just keep swinging and promise to stay focused on our goals.

11
Redemption

Life doesn't always give us a second chance to get things right. Sometimes our mistakes cause the kind of pain and suffering that is hard to undo. If we're lucky, though, we get an opportunity to show that we've learned from our mistakes and to redeem ourselves by making amends or reaching out and helping others. When those opportunities present themselves, I believe it's important to take action.

Because of two mistakes I made in the early part of my life, I am thankful to have learned a lesson that likely changed the path I was headed down. These mistakes also taught me the importance of integrity. I still get an intense feeling in the pit of my stomach when I reflect on those two events. That feeling is so powerful that the lessons learned continue to serve as reminders of how important it is for me to make choices based on what I know to be right in my heart and not just on the circumstances I find myself in.

The first incident happened when I was barely ten years old, not long after my father had lost his job and we found ourselves trying to get by on the little money that welfare provided. I had started hanging around the grocery stores in our neighborhood after school, hoping to earn tips from carrying customers' bags.

Because it was so busy, the huge A&P store not far from our home was usually the best bet for earning tips. Often four or five of us were vying to get to the customers first. I had an advantage over some of the others because, in addition to being small and quick (which allowed me to dart around the other kids), I also had seven siblings at home. Hunger fueled my determination.

"Hey, mister, you need a hand?" I asked one well-dressed man juggling shopping bags and a broom. Without a word, he handed me a couple of bags and the broom, and I followed him to his car.

"Look at me!" I called to the other kids, horsing around with the broom. I felt proud that I had won the first customer over them.

The man chuckled. "That's right son. Always walk tall and carry a big stick." He tipped me fifty cents and drove away.

The money trickled in—a quarter here, fifty cents there. By the time the store was preparing to close, I had enough to buy some lima beans, rice, milk, and even cereal for my younger brothers to have the next morning. I couldn't wait to get home to show my mother and to see the big fuss she was sure to make over my hard work and help to the family.

"Oh, my goodness," she said, smiling weakly at the packages I laid out on the table. She pulled out a pot and filled it with water to cook the beans. My excitement faded as my mother turned away, barely able to hide the shame and embarrassment over the fact that it had come to this: her ten-year-old son bringing home desperately needed food.

After that I spent most nights at the grocery store, hustling for whatever tips I could earn. That autumn turned into one of the coldest winters New York had ever experienced. We felt every degree of it in our unheated home—the electricity shut off when we didn't pay the bill— so every dollar I brought home made a difference.

As usual, on the day of the first incident, I was out in front of the grocery store from the time school let out until early evening. The problem on this particular night was that I wasn't making any tips, and it was getting late. Feeling frustrated and dejected, I decided to head over to a different store with another boy who was in the same situation. As we set off down the street, we spotted a young girl who was likely just a little younger than I walking toward us with what we were sure must be money clenched tightly in her hand. She was most likely on her way to pick up something at the store for her mother. Letting our desperation get the better of us, we stopped the girl, pried the ten dollar bill that she was carrying out of her hand, and ran off.

Although I was relieved to bring home food for my family that night, I was ashamed of how I had done it. The incident stuck in the pit of my stomach as something that should have never happened.

The situation that surrounded my second lapse in judgment also started out at the grocery store and took place a couple of months after the first. It was a cold January day. I was standing in front of the A&P hopping from foot to foot to keep warm as the sun faded from the sky, eagle-eyeing every customer who walked out of the swinging doors.

"Hey, mister, you need a hand?" I yelled after one middle-aged man who rumbled by with a shopping cart filled to the top with cartons of soda cans.

"Yep, as a matter of fact I do," he replied, motioning for me to follow him. "Hang on, I'll be back with my car," he said as he sprinted across the street to the parking lot, trusting that I would watch over his purchases. Middle Eastern looking and well groomed with a balding head, he was soft spoken but businesslike as we stacked the cases of soda into his car. "I'm going to need some help unloading these back at the Skylark Bar a few blocks up the road," he said. "Want to help?"

I knew the location of the bar because I passed it nearly every day. It was only a few blocks from our home. I also remember my parents going there when times were better. I hesitated for a moment. He seemed kind, gentle. I decided he was okay and hopped into his car.

He left me to unload the dozen or so cases in a storage room of his bar while he tended to his business. He asked if I wanted something to eat, instructing me to go into the kitchen and tell the cook to fix whatever I wanted. I thought for a moment that I must have died and gone to heaven.

"Grab a seat," he ordered when I came out with half a side of hot, juicy chicken from the deep fryer. I tore into the meat, listening to the friendly banter between him and the bartender while taking in my surroundings. With its jukebox, pool tables, and a bar that must have had a hundred different bottles of alcohol lined up on glass shelves, I was sure I was in the coolest place on earth.

If he knew that I was half starved, Sam didn't let on as he continued to talk to the bartender, seemingly unaware of my presence, but the moment I was done and wiped my mouth on my sleeve, he turned and smiled. "Want anything else?"

I did, but I knew enough not to press my luck. I didn't even expect a tip after the delicious meal I'd received.

"Hold up a minute," he yelled after me when I was halfway out the door. "What's your name?"

"My mom calls me Little Man," I said proudly.

"Well, Little Man, I have lots of odd jobs around here," he told me. "Stop by if you see my car out front." He pressed a five dollar bill into my hands. I couldn't believe my luck—even the tip was a small fortune to me.

After that, I regularly worked around Sam's bar, running errands for the cook, sweeping floors, and stacking empties. I liked everything about the Skylark. The men who came into the bar reminded me of Pop when he was working (most of them in dress shirts and pants with sharp creases). Whether it was busy or not, Sam and his staff always seemed to find something for me to do.

Sam, as it turned out, was a superb pool player. Around the bar's pool tables, everyone bet on shots. Wads of stacked bills teetered on the edge of the table, more money than I'd ever seen in my whole life.

"Let Little Man hold the money," Sam would tell the other players. After he won, he didn't even bother to count his winnings. Instead, he peeled off a handful of bills to give to me for holding the money.

About a month after I met Sam, I ran into him as he was leaving the bar. "I'm going home for a while," he said. "But I'll be back later." Suddenly his face brightened. "Hey, would it be okay with your parents if I took you home for supper?"

After a quick stop at my house to clear it with my parents, I was thrilled to be off on an adventure with Sam. Up to that point in time, my whole life had revolved around the streets of my neighborhood. I had never ventured beyond those few square blocks. Now Sam's car drove through the city, down the freeway, and out into suburbs that I never knew existed. I stared wide-eyed as we passed through street after street of beautiful homes with rolling green lawns.

Sam's home was neat and well cared for. Although I felt shy sitting in the dining room with his wife and daughters, they were warm, friendly, and interested in knowing more about me. While Sam took a nap, I watched TV with his family until it was time for him to drive me home.

The fact that Sam was generous to a fault, investing his trust in me and treating me as if I were part of his own family, made it all the more shameful when I eventually violated his trust.

The temptation presented itself the day I discovered Sam's hiding place for the till's float on a high cupboard shelf near his upstairs office. Putting away supplies in the cupboard, I came across several rolls of change, neatly stacked and organized by size. I stood for several minutes contemplating everything I could do with that much cash.

At the grocery store, no one had wanted me to carry out their groceries that day, and the thought of going home without any money or food was disheartening. I had come over to the bar hoping to earn some tips, but after completing the chores he had given me, Sam had been too busy and distracted to remember to pay me for my work. Now I had all the money I could ask for sitting right in front of me.

Feeling justified that I was only taking what Sam owed me (in essence, paying myself for that day's work), I reached in and curled my fingers around a heavy roll of quarters and a slim roll of dimes. Although it produced that same type of wrong feeling I had experienced when I stole the money from the little girl, instead of putting the money back, I slipped it into my pocket and closed the cupboard door.

I left the bar and headed straight to the grocery store to exchange the coins for paper money. Then, feeling rich, I walked into a White Castle restaurant to buy hamburgers for my entire family. The image of my parents—pleased and surprised that I had brought home such a lavish treat—filled my mind. As I counted out the money to pay for my order, I saw Sam's car pull up just outside the front door. My heart pounded in my chest. Somehow, he must have discovered the missing money, I thought, as I broke out in a sweat and my face flushed with heat.

"Hey! You're a rich little man today!" he joked, surveying the bags of hamburgers as he walked in the door. Shamefaced, I ducked my head, unable to meet his eyes.

"No, not really, not that much," I muttered as I grabbed my bags of food and hurried home.

About a week later, I mustered up enough nerve to go back to the Skylark where Sam greeted me cheerfully as if nothing at all had happened. As was his usual habit, he was playing pool and asked me to hold the money, tipping me handsomely afterward. Accepting the money, I felt unworthy and ashamed as I headed for the door. Unable to overcome my feelings of guilt or own up to what I had done, I never returned to Sam's bar. Although he never said a word to me about it, I'm convinced to this day that Sam knew everything.

> *Some things we have to learn the hard way!*

I felt sick in my heart for a long time after stealing the money from Sam. Both because I knew I had done something terribly wrong by stealing, but also because I had violated Sam's trust in me and destroyed a friendship that had become very important in my life. It was a hard lesson to learn, and it hurt like hell. I missed Sam terribly. I also missed the sense of hope and the feeling of protection I got when I was around him. I had messed up, made the same mistake twice, and didn't have anyone to blame but myself.

> *Guilt is the price we pay for the lessons*
> *that shape our character!*

I can live with myself if something I do hurts me. I can't live with myself if something I do hurts someone else or disappoints them. These two incidents really solidified my values and principles about respect for others.

Even though I would like to rewind time and take back what I did, I realize now that perhaps if those incidents hadn't happened at that point in my life, I would have headed down another path. Possibly I wouldn't have known enough to want to protect and preserve the trusting relationship I later established with Grandma Costa—which proved to be an important turning point in my life. They say everything happens for a reason. In this instance, I think that is true.

It's hard to forgive yourself for doing something you knew was wrong, but it is an essential part of learning and moving forward in your life. Guilt can be very debilitating. One thing I know as a result of all those experiences, when I put them all together I learned that I never wanted to be the kind of person who takes advantage of those who are trusting or vulnerable.

> *Sometimes we get a chance to redeem ourselves for the mistakes of the past!*

By the time Grandma Costa came into my life about a year after I last saw Sam, I had had plenty of time to think about my mistakes. Not only had I discovered the importance of having a strong character and doing the right thing, I had also determined the kind of life I wanted to lead—like Sam, I wanted to help others, not take advantage of them.

My friendship with Grandma Costa offered me the chance at redemption and the opportunity to right a wrong and release the burden of guilt I still carried over stealing from the little girl and Sam. I knew from the moment I met her I could never do anything to jeopardize her trust in me, and I never did. My relationship with Grandma Costa gave me the opportunity to put into action what I had learned from my experiences. She taught me that I could be trusted. I had learned my lesson.

When I reflect today on both Sam, the bar owner and Grandma Costa, I am convinced that they were each placed in my path for a reason. When I came upon them, I was losing hope. My life teetered precariously on the edge. I was ground down in an environment where failure and despair promised to play the most prominent role in my future. Little did I know that in many ways Sam and Grandma Costa would build a bridge to my survival. They were there to teach me, to love me, to give me support, hope, and encouragement during some critical stages of my life. Above all else, I believe they came into my life to prepare me for my journey to a new life.

Although they never made the journey with me, I have always carried them in my heart. I still do.

> *If you take from people, you deprive them of the opportunity to share with you.*

Now that I have children of my own, I'm using the lessons I learned from Sam and Grandma Costa in a new way—by passing them on to my two daughters. Just the other day I was ironing my clothes when my younger daughter came into the room and spotted some change on my desk.

"Whose money is this?" she asked, looking at the coins hopefully.

Seeing the expression on her face, I guessed she would have liked to have simply scooped it up and taken it for her piggy bank.

"That's my change," I told her. "But if you like, we can divide it up equally between you and your sister and put it in your piggy banks."

She skipped out of the room with a big smile on her face to find her sister and share the good news.

I felt immensely proud of her for asking first rather than just helping herself to the change. I reflected on how important it is, even within families where resources are shared, to have respect for each others' property. When we take things from others, we deprive them of the opportunity to share with us, and we take away the good feelings that come with being generous.

> *Redemption comes full circle!*

I recognized the significant guidance that Grandma Costa and my own grandmother provided to me. It was important for me to have "elders" in my life to help guide my own children. As a result of that desire, when Cheryl and I needed to find someone to help care for our first daughter, we were fortunate to have Liv and David

Sallows come into our life. At the time, Liv ran a daycare in her home, and David was a newly retired school principal.

With no extended family of our own nearby, over time, we grew very close to Liv and David, and they embraced us as if we were their own. By the time our second daughter came along, Cheryl and Liv had formed such a close bond that Liv stayed with her in the hospital room after Maxwell was born. Max has never known life without Liv and David. Even though Liv eventually retired from providing daycare in her home, it was made perfectly clear to us that she and David would not be relinquishing their roles as *Bestemor* (the Norwegian name for grandmother) and *Bestefar* (Norwegian for grandfather).

When I look at Liv and David and the relationship they have with our daughters, I can see that they are providing the same type of guidance I got from my own grandmother and from Grandma Costa. They are also a guiding light and a source of wisdom for both Cheryl and me. If ever I wondered if I have been blessed, the relationship I have with Liv and David tells me that I am—to me, it is a sign that redemption has come full circle in my life.

Promise to Make Amends and Forgive Yourself for Your Mistakes

Do good rather than feel bad. Dr. Fred Luskin, Director, Stanford University Forgiveness Project

It's never easy to admit when we've made a mistake, particularly if we knew what we were doing was wrong to begin with and it hurts someone we care about. The problem is that the alternative to owning up to our behavior and making amends for it can be far more damaging—if not for the person we have hurt, at least to ourselves. Knowing we have wronged someone (even if they are not aware of the wrong) often causes us to distance ourselves from that person—something that will usually destroy the relationship. In addition, when we don't step up and take responsibility for our actions, we diminish our sense of self-worth. The debilitating feelings of remorse and shame can eat away at us until we become emotionally or even physically ill.

It is important to make amends!

When we develop the courage to admit we have done something wrong and work past our resistance to making amends, there is an opportunity to re-establish our sense of self-respect. Apologizing or making amends helps us to remain emotionally connected to the people we respect and care about. Also, the act of admitting our mistakes usually causes us to feel humiliated and humbled, which can be a good deterrent and, at the same time, remind us not to get caught up in that kind of behavior in the future.

Turn your guilt into something positive to help you move forward!

Replaying what you did over and over again in your head isn't going to help you or the person you hurt. It just makes you feel bad. We can't change what we did in the past, but we can channel the guilt into positive action.

It's not enough to say you're sorry!

Too many people seem to believe they can behave terribly as long as they're willing to apologize afterward. They don't see the importance of refraining from repeating the same mistakes in the future. Sorry means nothing if it is not accompanied by a change in behavior. The word *amend* actually means to make a change, and that is what we need to do after we have admitted our mistake. Making amends—whether it is returning or replacing something we took or damaged, going to counselling to reconcile the harm we have done to a relationship, or doing community work as compensation—provides us with the opportunity to turn our negative behavior into something positive by applying what we have learned and working to repair the damage. Even if the person we hurt is no longer a part of our life, we can still make up for our behavior by helping and showing kindness to others. In religious terms, it's often called atonement, and atonement involves making an offering of our time, money, or effort to someone who needs it to demonstrate our desire for forgiveness and redemption.

Forgive yourself and let go of the guilt!

The next step after making amends to others is to forgive ourselves for our mistakes. Although there is a tendency in all of us to hold ourselves more accountable than we do others, if we can't forgive ourselves, we can't move on. We end up stuck in the past and closed off from opportunity. With forgiveness comes healing. Once we begin to heal, we open up our life to new possibilities, and we start to move forward again.

An important part of being able to forgive ourselves is understanding that we all make mistakes, and mistakes are part of learning and growing. We don't need to be punished (even by guilt) as much as we need to learn from our experience. If you've been unable to forgive yourself for something that you have made amends for, most likely it's because you are holding yourself up to an impossible standard. Cut yourself some slack and remember that we're all human; we all have lapses in judgment and that is how we learn many of those important life lessons (the ones that shape our character and make us more compassionate toward others). In seeking redemption, we allow the lessons we have learned to help us become a person of integrity, willing to admit our shortcomings and always striving to do better. To become such a person, we must promise to make amends and forgive ourselves for our mistakes.

12

Promises to Keep: The Power of One to Make a Difference

I am inspired by people who strive to make a difference. These are people who understand that we all share this planet together and that it is up to us to work to make it a better place for future generations—to put our best talents to work, individually and collectively.

I have discovered one of the most positive things from doing speaking engagements from coast to coast: individuals and community-based groups doing wonderful things and making a difference in the world. America's Promise Alliance is close to my heart because of what they have undertaken to accomplish and the enormity of their commitment.

Originally founded just over a decade ago with Colin Powell as chair, the Alliance (which partners with organizations all over the U.S.) is dedicated to keeping five promises to the youth of America. Each of the promises focuses on one developmental resource that every child needs to be successful in life. The five promises are caring adults, safe places, a healthy start, effective education, and opportunities to help others. On their tenth anniversary in 2007, the Alliance unveiled their *15 in 5 Campaign Network* aimed at reaching out to 15 million of America's most disadvantaged youth within the next five years and providing them with more of the supports that underscore the five promises.

> *Put yourself in the picture to make a difference!*

Here's what I love about the Alliance and the many, many other organizations that focus on solving the most significant problems in our world today. They demonstrate in a very real way how each of us has the power to make a difference. All we need to do to make that happen is to "put ourselves in the picture." We've talked about this concept before in terms of how it can help us to "imagine the best," but now I'd like to elaborate on it a bit more to show how significant putting yourself in the picture can be in turning thoughts and ideas into action.

My benefactors put themselves in the picture when they made the decision to ask me to come and live with them in Toronto. But what motivated them to do such a thing? Why would they want to pull some kid out of the ghetto and bring him into their home? It's a question that I'm sure a lot of you have asked yourself. Why not simply offer to help out the family financially or donate to a charity that helps inner-city kids?

The answer, the reason they reached out to help me in such a personal way is that this was an idealistic group of people, hippies really, with a strong social conscience, who shared a deeply held belief that we all have a responsibility to help one another. They also believed that it is the responsibility of every community to nurture and teach children and to prepare them to be productive members of society so that they in turn are able to make a contribution and help others.

Living communally, working together, and sharing their resources, my benefactors were absolutely passionate about living up to their ideals. Knowing that they had the means and the ability to help me, they felt it was their duty to act on their convictions—and I'm forever grateful that they did. As old-fashioned and simplistic as it may seem, I think their philosophy that we have a responsibility to help those who come into our path is an important one. We should all embrace it.

> *Don't let fear hold you back!*

I believe that most of us dream of a better world, but when it comes to going further and taking action, we often don't know where to start, or we allow our fear to get in the way. I describe this fear in many ways: fear that we're not powerful enough to make a difference, fear that helping others will diminish the resources we have for ourselves, fear that the problems we see around us are too monumental, fear that our kindness will be taken advantage of, fear that if we fail we will lose the respect of others, or fear that we won't be up to the task. With this cloud of fear hovering over us, it is far easier to hold back and do nothing.

| *Small gestures can have a big impact!* |

You don't have to be rich like Bill and Melinda Gates or a famous personality like Oprah to make a difference in the world. Putting yourself in the picture is about taking action even if you're not completely sure what to do. It's about taking small steps forward, following what your heart tells you is right, and letting your instincts guide you.

A little difference can go a long way. What may seem like a small gesture to you could have a great impact on someone else's life. Remember the story about Simon Hailey and the man on the train? What was likely not a lot of money to the elderly passenger changed Simon's life by providing him with the means to continue his education and lift his family out of poverty. That small kindness continued to pay dividends into the next generation as each of Simon's children received an education and achieved success in the world including the well-known writer, Alex Hailey.

Small doors can sometimes lead into big rooms. In my own life, although it might have seemed like a small thing to her, by paying me to assist her with errands and chores, Grandma Costa was helping to support my entire family at a time when we really needed it. As a result, she gave me hope that a better future existed for me.

By putting yourself in the picture and reaching out to others, you too can make a difference. Small gestures have the power to change lives. When you begin to add together the little acts of kindness that individuals like the man on the train and Grandma Costa have made, it becomes much easier to see how it is possible to change the world.

To me, the marvels and miracles that we witness every day are testimony to the power of individuals not only to dream, but to turn those dreams into concrete action. But it takes determination. No marvels, no miracles, would be possible were it not for the determination of people who said, "I can do this!' "I have the ability to make a difference, and I am going to make the best use of the resources at hand to make a contribution."

Even if we don't know where to start or we're afraid to venture out on our own, there are plenty of like-minded people and organizations in every community that would be more than happy to welcome our contribution. We should never underestimate the compounding effect of putting your hand together with others. When you put yourself in the picture, when you reach out to others and ask, "How can I help?" wonderful things begin to happen both in your life and in the lives of the people you touch.

> *Lend a hand where you can!*

I am blessed with the opportunity to travel to many places in the world today. In my travels, I am moved by the common desire that so many people possess to make a difference.

Unfortunately, many others who could make a contribution have given up. They think the world has become too polluted, too bureaucratic, or too focused on money and power for their efforts to end up as anything more than a drop in the bucket. What they have lost sight of is that we all share a responsibility to build the community, the country, and the world that we want. When we don't do our part—and others in turn don't do their part, it has a domino effect, and our world becomes a poorer place for it.

There's an old saying that it takes a community to raise a child. It's true. It takes the strength of an entire community working together to provide the support, discipline, and love that is required for a child to grow up in the kind of safe, nurturing environment we all want for our children.

Imagine trying to teach your children to be strong, respectful, and hardworking when they are surrounded by violence, substance abuse, and poverty. Imagine having to live in a neighborhood like that because it is all you can afford. Imagine sending your child to school every day and then discovering at age fifteen that your child cannot read or write. Imagine strangers knocking on your door and asking to take your child away. Even if in your heart you knew that letting your child go would give him or her a better life than you could provide, could you do it?

That's the question my mother and father faced. My mother was so distraught at the idea that she couldn't answer. Jumping up from her seat she told my benefactors, "I can't make that decision. You can't ask me to give up my son." Leaving the room to try and calm down, she turned to my father and told him, "Earl, you have to decide."

Imagine having to make that choice. I cannot conceive of a more selfless act than giving up your child, even if it is to provide him or her with a better opportunity. I am thankful every day that my parents could be so brave, but when I reflect on the reason behind it, I have to tell you I get angry. Angry because I was born in the land of opportunity and my parents should not have had to be so brave. Angry because there is no reason why a mother, a citizen of one of the world's mightiest nations, should have to even conceive of giving up a child in order to provide that child with a proper education. Angry because we cannot afford to let millions of young minds go undeveloped.

My goal is to ensure that no mother should have to make the decision my mother faced, and that goal is what inspires me to keep on going, to do today what needs to be done and to share with you the message that we all have the power to make a difference in the world.

On an individual basis we can have a significant impact. Imagine the effect of every person who can read taking the time to teach someone who can't. If every individual who has the resources invested in one person who doesn't, the dividends would far exceed anything that anyone could ever imagine, and the world would be a different place. We need to invest ourselves in taking care of each other so that we can educate, nurture, and inspire the next generation with the knowledge that anything is possible as long as they commit to putting themselves in the picture.

To make that happen we need to figure out a way to be more connected together. When I first met my benefactors, the relationship that we built was a human one. If they hadn't been willing to take the time to get to know me, they would never have been moved to rescue me from the ghetto. Likewise, if they hadn't been there to encourage and support me when I was struggling with the demons of my past and wanted to give up, my life today would be very, very different, I am sure of it.

Knowing when the people around us need our assistance or how best to help them can be harder to figure out in a world where more and more of our interactions with others take place electronically. In our busy, technology-enhanced lives, we need to look for opportunities to connect with others. We need to get out of our cars and take the time to walk and talk with the people in our neighborhood. We need to keep reaching out and building those human relationships that remind us of what we can accomplish when we help one another. I challenge you to lend a hand where you can.

Promise to Use Your Power to Make a Difference

All labor that uplifts humanity has dignity and importance and should be undertaken with painstaking excellence.
Martin Luther King

I have addressed a lot of audiences, and one thing I know for sure is that we all want to make a difference, a contribution, and we all wonder if we ever have or can. After you read this book, my hope is that you are going to do more than wonder. I want you to believe that each one of us can make a difference. We have the power and we can believe in our own abilities. Like the little engine that could, sometimes we need to focus on the simplest and most powerful force in our lives: *I think I can, I think I can, I know I can, I know I can. I can do it if I just believe in me.*

We all have something to contribute!

As I mentioned earlier, when I overcame my problem with reading and writing, all of a sudden I had not only physical freedom, but also intellectual freedom—to look beyond my own situation and realize that I had something to offer the world. As a result, I began to take time to reflect on the issues that affected my community, to take the time to respond to the concerns of others, and to take the time to reach out and connect with people in a meaningful way, to share my story, become a leader, and inspire leadership in others.

John D. Rockefeller once said, "I believe that every right implies a responsibility; every opportunity, an obligation; every possession, a duty." Blessed with the ability to live in a democratic society, we all have the power to make a difference and a responsibility to contribute what we can. Isn't that what my benefactors did for me? They didn't have to offer me a chance. They could have simply enjoyed the times that we had together while they were doing their business in New York and left things at that. But they didn't. They stopped and extended an opportunity to me because they could, because they believed that we are all our brother's and sister's keepers. Each one of us has an obligation to do the same to the extent that we can.

Out of respect for the people who sacrificed and fought for both the rights and the lifestyle that many of us enjoy today, we should be especially committed to making sure that those who have fallen through the cracks or been excluded be provided with the same access to a good education and employment opportunities as we have had.

We need to get back to basics and lend a hand where we can!

Not long ago in this country, people took care of each other. Everybody in the community looked out for the children who lived there, and young people grew up with a sense of pride and belonging. These are the principles that form the foundation of our society. In my own neighborhood, I remember one lady in particular who took this responsibility very seriously. Her name was Mrs. Brown, and she lived a few doors down from my family. She was the mama watchdog in our neighborhood. She made no bones about any of us knowing that she was watching, that she was our elder, and that she had no qualms about being a moral authority in the neighborhood.

The most amazing thing to us kids was just how much she saw and how quick on her feet she was. Whenever Mrs. Brown spotted any of us kids doing something we shouldn't, she would march right out from her place by the window in her first-floor apartment, come right up to us, and pop us upside the head so fast that we didn't even see it coming. She wasn't afraid to dish out the punishment, and while she was doing it, she would make it clear that as soon as our mother got home, she would know that we were up to no good (and we could always be sure that she would intercept our mom even before she walked through the door; it was spooky).

We could also be sure that when mother got home, no questions asked, she would wail into us for doing the things Mrs. Brown had reported to her.

Today, we would be outraged if neighbors took it upon themselves to chastise one of our children the way Mrs. Brown did when I was a kid (even without the smack upside the head). Many parents would even go so far as to call the authorities or threaten a lawsuit. Yet my parents and the other parents in the neighborhood were grateful to her.

We need to get back to those basics, to a time when the whole community took responsibility for raising children, back to focusing on what makes a community feel like home, back to respecting our public spaces, back to feeling connected with one another—and we can start by making a commitment to lend a hand where we can. Even if we don't have a lot of time or specific skills to offer, we can start with small gestures. We all have something to share, and every little bit counts. Whether we choose to reach out to help a neighbor, volunteer in the community, coach children's sports, mentor young adults, or organize a neighborhood get-together, everything we contribute will make a difference in someone's life.

Become an agent of change!

A lot of people get down with worrying about what is happening in the world. They focus on the bad news and start to think there is nothing to be done, that any effort they make will simply be inconsequential next to all of the bad things that happen. That's the message I often get from people who attend my presentations. People tell me they don't believe they can make a difference or that there is no point in even trying unless it is to do something on such a grand scale that it would change the lives of a whole lot of people. And because they can't do that, they do nothing. However, in doing nothing, they discount the incredible power we have to make a difference one step and one person at a time.

Each of us has the power to help paste the world back together again. Our awareness and sensitivity to the imbalances of the world should not depress us; instead, they should inspire us to become agents of change, to speak up for what we believe in, and to challenge accepted notions that are limiting or harmful.

Although significant changes often happen more slowly than we would like them to, they are almost never the result of one person acting alone, and they don't happen at all until enough people are willing to speak up and take action.

Believe in the power of putting yourself in the picture!

All it takes for us to begin to make a difference is the ability to put ourselves in the picture and to step up and offer a hand. Shortly before his death in 2003, former Illinois senator Paul Simon, a man who spent his entire life serving others, wrote a book called *Fifty-two Simple Ways to Make a Difference* in which he outlined scores of practical things that each of us can do. In that book, he said, "All of us should become giraffes, people who are willing to stick out their necks to help others." I like the image and I like the sentiment, because in sticking our necks out we undoubtedly expose a vulnerable part of ourselves. However, at the same time, we have the opportunity to see sights above and beyond what those who choose to keep their heads down will ever experience.

Lesra Martin

Promises to Keep

Each one of us has promises, like these, to keep to the next generation:

- To offer hope for those who are struggling
- To demonstrate the importance of letting our heart lead the way
- To show how human spirit can overcome great obstacles
- To inspire others to dream of how they too can make a difference
- To prove that with a little discipline, incredible things can be accomplished

With all the resources, imagination, and determination we possess, we have the ability to create the brighter future we all want for our children. All we need to do to make it happen is to promise to use our power to make a difference.

The power is within you!

From the bottom of my heart, thank you for taking the time to read this book. I hope my story will remind you that the actions of one person can indeed have an impact on the world. The power to make a difference exists in each and every one of us. It's up to you and me to harness that power and use it to change the world.

Conclusion
The Worst Kind of Prison

I was raised in one of the poorest neighborhoods in the United States. I found my freedom through reading. The reality that there are still so many people today who don't know how huge the world is, or how magnificent it can be, because they cannot read, is an indescribable tragedy that we should all dedicate ourselves in some way to overcoming.

What is illiteracy if not a type of prison? In my opinion, it is no different from prison in its capacity to rob individuals of their dignity and sense of hope for the future. For me, illiteracy was even worse than being locked up in jail, because I felt I was locked away in my own mind.

When I was fifteen and first discovered that I couldn't read or write, I became despondent. Not realizing that my illiteracy was the product of a flawed education system, I was burdened with the thought that I was incapable of learning.

Later, when working with a tutor, I discovered that I had been fooled into believing I could read because I could pick out one or two primary words. As I sat with my tutor, I would look at words on the page, desperately trying to find ones I recognized, like *cat* or *dog*. I would then make up stories from these few simple words. I thought that was "reading."

The nuts and bolts of learning to read are only one part of the equation. Without the proper encouragement and nurturing of the mind, too many kids will never reach their full potential. I once stood before my tenth-grade class in Bed-Stuy. It was career day, and we were supposed to tell the rest of the class our plans. I stood up and announced that I wanted to become a lawyer. After a long, uncomfortable pause, my teacher leaned over and whispered, "You need to do something more realistic with your life. Learn a trade, be a garbage man, do something with your hands." Her comments crushed me.

After I left Bed-Stuy with a group of do-gooders and went to live—and study—in Toronto, my tutor used just about everything he could to motivate me to learn. He would often say, "Write something from your heart, tell me what you feel," but the page remained blank. It wasn't until I found Rubin Carter's autobiography, *The 16th Round,* and read about his struggle to right an injustice and regain his freedom that I felt moved enough to find my own voice and the inspiration to learn.

I gained an invaluable lesson from reading about Rubin's unjust imprisonment: No matter what people take away from you physically, they can't take away what you've learned. And that's when I truly began to learn. Ironically, I would help free Rubin from a physical prison and through his story, Rubin helped to free me from the prison of illiteracy.

When I speak to audiences about literacy and the importance of giving every child the benefit of a good education, I like to remind them that we learn not just with our minds, but with our hearts. The world is not fair; it can be cruel, and we don't determine the hand we get dealt. Millions of young people live in neighborhoods just like mine. They have not been as fortunate as I. That's why it's so important to give encouragement and support wherever possible, because as my story shows, when you help someone find the key that unlocks that prison door, suddenly the whole world opens up for that person. They, in turn, are inspired to open doors for others.

About the Author

Of his eight siblings, Lesra is the only one with a high school diploma. He completed high school as an Ontario scholar in 1983 and received an Honours B.A. from the University of Toronto in 1988. He achieved his law degree from Dalhousie Law School in 1997 and served as a Prosecutor in Kamloops, BC. He and his lawyer wife, Cheryl now have their own law firm, **Martin & Martin Lawyers**, in British Columbia.

Lesra has built a dynamic speaking career that enables him to travel throughout North America. "The power to make a difference exists in each of us," he tells audiences. He has spread his message of hope to thousands, appearing before corporate groups, community organizations, schools and universities. He has appeared as a keynote speaker for a wide variety of companies and organizations, including IBM, General Motors, Hewlett-Packard and the International Subway Corporation. He has delivered his heart felt message to Piney Woods School (Mississippi), Atlanta International School, Boston College, Baylor University and Dartmouth, as well as appearing before the Mel Goldberg Symposium on Justice (Minnesota), Council of Exceptional Children (Child Development Institute, Early Literacy), and the YMCA (Ohio) among many others.

Lesra was invited to speak before the General Assembly delegates at the United Nations, where he gave an impassioned speech about the devastating effects of literacy and poverty, and at Cambridge University, where he spoke before world leaders.

His life was featured, in part, in the major motion Hollywood film, "The Hurricane," starring Denzel Washington. He has also been featured on countless television and radio shows, most notably as a special guest on *The Oprah Winfrey Show* and *Larry King Live*. Dozens of newspaper and magazines articles from *The New York Times* and *The Washington Post* to *Sports Illustrated* and *Reader's Digest Magazine* have chronicled aspects of Lesra's life.

Inspired by his experiences, The National Film Board of Canada produced the documentary "*The Journey of Lesra Martin*," and the compelling film has been screened at film festivals throughout Canada as well as the *Hollywood Black Film Festival, Black Film Festival* (San Francisco), *The Urban Literary Film Festival* (Greensboro, North Carolina) and the *24th International Durban Film Festival* (Durban, South Africa).

Lesra has received YMCA Black Achievers Partner in Excellence Award (Ohio). He has received numerous awards and certificates of recognition for his willingness to be a role model and mentor for youth. He was acknowledged with a lifetime membership with the National Black Caucus of Special Educators, a division of the CEC (Washington, D.C.).